T0326736

A Map of
Longings

A Map of Longings

The Life and Works of
Agha Shahid Ali

MANAN KAPOOR

Yale UNIVERSITY PRESS
NEW HAVEN AND LONDON

First published in the United States by Yale University Press in 2023.
First published in India by Penguin Random House India in 2021.

Yale University Press books may be purchased in quantity for educational,
business, or promotional use. For information, please e-mail sales.press@yale.edu
(U.S. office) or sales@yaleup.co.uk (U.K. office).

Typeset in Adobe Caslon Pro by Manipal Technologies Limited, Manipal.
Printed in the United States of America.

Library of Congress Control Number: 2022941448
ISBN 978-0-300-26422-7 (hardcover : alk. paper)

A catalogue record for this book is available from the British Library.

This paper meets the requirements of ANSI/NISO Z39.48-1992 (Permanence of
Paper).

10 9 8 7 6 5 4 3 2 1

To the memory of Agha Ashraf Ali

Contents

Illustrations follow page 166.

Preface

A Map of Longings: The Life and Works of Agha Shahid Ali was first published in the Indian subcontinent in June 2021. Like all other genres, biography is expansive, and biographers take different approaches to exploring their subjects. To discuss my reasons for writing this biography and to review the aspects of Agha Shahid Ali's life and works I hoped to examine, I included an introduction. Although in the Indian subcontinent Shahid is a major English-language poet who does not require a formal introduction, for readers across the globe I felt that certain aspects of his life and work needed to be illuminated. No changes have been made in this edition, but I have added this preface to clarify the extent and scope of the biography for readers worldwide and to address questions that might come up as they engage with Shahid's life and works.

First and foremost, this is a literary biography, in which I illuminate the life of a poet and the forces that shaped his work. My primary aim with this biography was to make readers more conversant with Shahid's poetry and shed light on his poetic concerns and approaches. In the biography, I return to Shahid's body of poetry and its cultural roots in various parts of the world—from Kashmir, New Delhi, to the American south-west and Massachusetts, to name a few—and to the people who shaped his political, cultural, and personal milieu in order to map the trajectory of his poetic career. While my primary concern in all the interviews I conducted was the interaction between Shahid's life and work, his approach towards his craft was a subject that came up often. Shahid weaved his poetic vision and approach into day-to-day conversations, and I explore this aspect of his practice. In the biography, I discuss Shahid's poetic methods and the ways in which they evolved. Readers will find early drafts of poems such as 'The Dacca Gauzes', analyses of the techniques he employed and his views on literary forms, aesthetics and politics in poetry. They will meet Shahid as a poet who constantly challenged himself as well as others around him. I hope that the material from which he created some of his poems, the anecdotes that speak of his dedication to poetry, and his conversations with other poets, academics and writers will serve as a significant contribution to our understanding of the man as well as his work.

Readers who are familiar with Shahid's poetry are aware that he traversed many geographies, cultures, religions, and traditions in his poems and that a global literary bricolage shaped his poetics. Shahid's transnationalism is undoubtedly one of the most important aspects of his work. In his book *A Transnational Poetics*, Jahan Ramazani looks at how 'transnational templates' such as 'globalization, migration, travel, genre, influence, modernity, decolonization, and diaspora . . . indicate the many ways in which modern and contemporary poetry in English overflows national borders, exceeding the scope of national literary paradigms.'[1] Shahid's poetry responds to almost all the 'transnational templates' that Ramazani offers. Even a cursory reading exposes Shahid's position as a migrant postcolonial poet in the twentieth century and reveals the presence in his works of multiple cultures and religions (Islam, Hinduism, Christianity, and others), languages (English, Kashmiri, Urdu), and regions (America and the Indian subcontinent), as well as the crucial influence of other poets (Faiz Ahmad Faiz, Mirza Ghalib, T.S. Eliot, Osip Mandelstam, Emily Dickinson, and James Merrill, to name a few). While it was challenging to navigate these cross-cultural affiliations and influences, I hope that with the help of this biography readers worldwide will come to recognize the plurality that Shahid's poetry epitomizes and will find they can traverse Shahid's multitudes with ease. I also hope these aspects of Shahid's world will help readers gain perspective on how poetry transcends borders via processes such as translation, migration, influence, and travel, which are central to the world of literary studies today.

Shahid's life intersected with movements such as the conflict and violence in his homeland, Kashmir, and the AIDS crisis in America. Other pivotal events such as the partition of the Indian subcontinent shaped his environment. I discuss how political and cultural movements and events such as the execution of Julius and Ethel Rosenberg—which his parents discussed at his home in Kashmir—remained with Shahid and informed his poetic outlook. While I have described these events in some detail, it was impossible to shed light on their myriad aspects within the scope of this book. I do look at crucial events that led to poems, such as the Bisbee Deportation of 1917—of which, surprisingly, even most Americans I know were unaware. Shahid's collection *The Country without a Post Office* was a response to the conflict in Kashmir, and in chapter 14 I provide a précis of the ongoing violence and political turmoil in the region. Naturally, a few pages cannot do justice to all that has taken place in Kashmir, and interested readers will find works that discuss Kashmir's political history in greater detail cited in the notes. For the benefit of non-South Asian readers, I identify unfamiliar terms and references to customs, traditions, and rituals of the Indian subcontinent in the text.

Shahid moved from city to city, from one place to another over the course of his life and was at home in all these locations— not just Kashmir or New Delhi but also Massachusetts, Arizona, New York, and Pennsylvania. I discuss the relationships that informed the way he thought and dreamt in each of these phases of his life and how he shaped the worldview of the people around him as a friend, as a teacher and most importantly as a poet. Poets, musicians, and artists who helped shape Shahid's imagination, including James Merrill, Begum Akhtar, Faiz Ahmad Faiz, Eqbal Ahmad, and Edward Said, appear in this biography. In addition to showing how they influenced Shahid's life and work, I hope to introduce readers to their own work. Although I explore all the relationships, experiences and events that informed Shahid's poetic outlook in detail, certain aspects of his private life and personal environment that were extraneous and exceeded the purview and scope of this biography have not been discussed.

Since this is a biography of a poet, the most important questions for me were those about language. 'I write in English—and I have always written in English,' Shahid once said.[2] As a postcolonial poet from the subcontinent, however, Shahid was aware of the problems of writing in English and especially of the inadequacies of the language for a South Asian poet. In the late seventies, soon after he moved to America to take his graduate degree at Penn State, Shahid wrote in an essay that 'English in India has a formal, stilted quality. It does not breathe the Indian air,' and he added that no poet had 'changed and re-created the language' and that 'genuine poetry' in the language would arise only if the language became 'sufficiently Indianized'.[3] By the nineties, he had allowed his experience as a South Asian to affect his diction and syntax, reconceptualizing his approach and using an Urdu-inflicted English. Ultimately, it was how he contended with the language and its inadequacies that made him stand apart from most South Asian English-language poets. His life in the United States, however, had much to do with his recognition and awareness of the language he called his own.

As I traced the development of his language, a few questions came up frequently. Would Shahid have translated the poetry of Faiz Ahmad Faiz if he had never left the subcontinent? There is enough evidence to suggest that he translated Faiz primarily because of Faiz's absence from the American literary landscape and that translating the works of the Pakistani poet ultimately transformed how Shahid approached his own poems. It allowed him to understand nuances of both Urdu and English and helped him incorporate the sensibilities, mannerisms, and themes of Urdu poetics into English. Had he stayed in the subcontinent would he have attempted to write ghazals in English, a feat for which he is celebrated in the West? He did so after reading the ghazals of Adrienne Rich, Jim Harrison, and Phyllis Webb; though he might have responded to them from the Indian subcontinent, I suspect that he would not have engaged with their work so passionately, since the distance from a poetic form he had grown up with sharpened his concerns. America, then, becomes an important place for him as a poet, and it is hardly a surprise that he claimed he was a poet with 'dual loyalties' to 'two cultures, both of which I felt in my bones' and that he chose to call himself a 'Kashmiri-American' poet—the designation he chose for his epitaph.[4]

Although 'Kashmiri-American' is the term that has come to define Shahid today, even towards the end of his life Shahid claimed that he had never been interested in designations. Shahid stated on several occasions that the only designation he accepted without any qualms was that of an English-language poet. In an interview, he listed all the hyphenations that could be used instead of 'Kashmiri-American': Indian-American, South Asian-American, Muslim-American, and so on, and said: 'All of those designations would be true, in one way or the other, and if they're used in larger ways, I don't have an objection to them. But if they're used simply to restrict me, I'm not interested in them.'[5]

Though he weaved many cultural, political, and geographic strands that were integral to his upbringing into his poems, as a poet Shahid refused to be a spokesperson for any ideology or group. He once said in an interview: 'I want people to respond to me as an individual poet trying like other poets to charge language to its utmost. So that is why I refuse . . . to "represent" Kashmir, or India or Islam.'[6] In another interview, Shahid stated that the moment a poet becomes a spokesperson, they start 'a kind of dumbing down', wherein the poet might come to say: 'Now I am a spokesman, I want to be understood by all and sundry. So I don't now have to expect much from my audience'; Shahid considered such an attitude 'condescending'.[7] Shahid claimed to have taken the same approach to the relationship between his sexuality and his poetry.

Several people and relationships shape a poet's work, and poets are especially affected by their partners. Whether it is the presence of David Jackson or Peter Hooten in James Merrill's life or that of Lota de Macedo Soares in Elizabeth Bishop's, we see that a poet's partner reveals much about their personality. While I raised questions about Shahid's partners in all my interviews, I did not uncover any long-term partners or lovers of Shahid. It has been more than twenty years since Shahid's death, and no one has claimed to have been his lover, nor did my interviews with his friends, family, colleagues and fellow poets reveal any names of people who might have been involved with him. I was thus unable to speak with anyone who was in a relationship with Shahid, however briefly. With such a dearth of information about Shahid's private life, I found it difficult to gauge the degree to which his sexuality influenced his poetry—especially since Shahid himself claimed that his sexuality was a private aspect of his life which did not interest him as a poet.

There is no ambiguity about his sexual orientation—he was gay. He lived during the AIDS crisis, at a time when there was much more discrimination and prejudice against homosexuality than today, in both India and America. My interviews, however, suggested that Shahid was comfortable with his sexuality throughout his life. From what I could gather, Shahid had no qualms about his sexual orientation, a matter I discuss in detail in chapter 7. He claimed on many occasions that his poetry was unencumbered as far as his sexual life was concerned; he had no sexual angst which he wished to express through his work. In one of his final interviews, however, he added that he might unconsciously have incorporated his sexuality into his poems, as he had done with other aspects of his personal life, but it wasn't something he wanted to pursue actively there. In the biography I discuss all that I could identify or that Shahid spoke about concerning his sexuality, such as his use of pronouns in his poems.

Once, when asked why he didn't talk about his sexuality as a poet, he said that he didn't want it to be the 'central element' of his identity; the primary importance for him as a poet was the work itself, and one's background was 'finally very boring' to him as a writer.[8] Shahid even refused on multiple occasions to let his poems be included in anthologies of gay poetry because he wanted them to be 'recognized, appreciated, or even disliked . . . as work,' and not because he had a particular background or sexual orientation.[9] In an interview, he claimed that although one's background, ethnicity, or sexual orientation could be a 'convenient tool' when it came to poetry, he wasn't interested in it. *Convenience* was for him a 'dirty word'. Even when he agreed with the politics of any particular issue, he saw 'people turning it into something easy for themselves. Something black and white, something convenient, and something irritating.'[10] This refusal to be 'convenient' and his resistance to any attempts to be categorized make him a complex and interesting subject for a biographer, for while they veil some aspects of his private life, they reveal that as a poet, above all else his loyalty was to language.

Throughout the biography, I refer to the poet as Shahid. While I am aware that using the first name suggests a personal closeness to the subject that I did not have, this was a conscious decision. His family called him Bhaiya, but everybody else I interviewed remembered him as Shahid. In earlier drafts of this biography, I used his last name, Ali, but over time I realized that it was only right to call him Shahid since he had so intricately woven his name into his poetics. He once said that there were two central aspects of his poetry: the act of witnessing ('I know there has always been a political element in my life') and that of being the beloved ('having been in love and having been loved, and having found a lot of satisfaction and fullness through it'),[11] both of which stemmed from

his name. He writes about them in the final couplet of his ghazal
'In Arabic':

> They ask me to tell them what Shahid means: Listen, listen:
> It means 'The Beloved' in Persian, 'witness' in Arabic.[12]

I hope that readers will encounter both these facets in their
fullness throughout this biography and will meet him as Shahid,
a poet who bore witness to injustices around the world; a poet
whose verses evoke the longing for the beloved; and finally, a poet
in search of a home in the intricacies of language, where his legacy
now remains.

Notes

1. Jahan Ramazani, 'Preface', *A Transnational Poetics* (Chicago: University of Chicago Press, 2015), p. xi.
2. Eric Gamalinda, 'Poems Are Never Finished: A Final Interview with Agha Shahid Ali', *Poets & Writers*, March–April 2002, p. 47.
3. Agha Shahid Ali, 'Indian Poetry in English', box 3, folder 1, Special Collections at Hamilton College, Burke Library, Hamilton College, Clinton, New York, p. 3.
4. Agha Shahid Ali, 'Introduction', *The Rebel's Silhouette: Selected Poems* (Amherst: University of Massachusetts Press, 1995), p. xxi.
5. Christian Benvenuto, 'Interview with Agha Shahid Ali', *Massachusetts Review*, vol. 43, no. 2, Summer, 2002, p. 267.
6. Lawrence Needham, 'Interview with Agha Shahid Ali', *The Verse Book of Interviews: 27 Poets on Language, Craft & Culture*, ed. Brian Henry and Andrew Zawacki (Seattle: Wave Books, 2005), p. 140.
7. Heather Marring, 'Conversation with Agha Shahid Ali', *Center: A Journal of the Literary Arts*, February 2002, p. 60.
8. Eric Gamalinda, 'Poems Are Never Finished: A Final Interview with Agha Shahid Ali', p. 48.
9. Ibid.
10. Heather Marring, 'Conversation with Agha Shahid Ali', p. 60.
11. Eric Gamalinda, 'Poems Are Never Finished: A Final Interview with Agha Shahid Ali', p. 47.

12. Agha Shahid Ali, 'In Arabic', *The Veiled Suite: The Collected Poems* (New Delhi: Penguin Random House, 2010), p. 372.

Introduction

My first formal encounter with poetry happened through my mother, who, looking at the lilies that bloomed in our garden each spring, quoted from T.S. Eliot's 'The Waste Land': 'April is the cruellest month, breeding / Lilacs out of the dead land, mixing / memory and desire.'[1] But it could also very well have been through the renditions of the ghazals of Mirza Ghalib that my father played so often. I cannot recall which came first, but the magical presence of poetry during my formative years had caused a wound. This wound opened itself once again in my teenage years when I first read a poem by Agha Shahid Ali.

I vividly remember reading poems like 'A Rehearsal for Loss', 'Stationery' and his famous one-liners, 'Suicide Note' and 'On Hearing a Lover Not Seen for Twenty Years Has Attempted Suicide' (a poem whose title is longer than the body), and marvelling at the sheer simplicity and clarity—there was something ineffable about his language that instantly took a hold of me. Years later, I was informed by his brother, Agha Iqbal Ali, that Shahid had singled out some short poems like 'Stationery' as crowd-pleasers that he would open his readings with to charm the audience. The trick had worked on me, and over the next few years, the more I read, the more Shahid reeled me in.

I could also say, at the risk of romanticizing the past, that I became aware of Shahid at just the right moment, when I was ready for him. The years leading up to my first novel, *The Lamentations of a Sombre Sky*, were also the years of my political coming of age. Throughout my bachelor's degree, I was working on a novel set in Srinagar in the early '90s. Although I read numerous accounts of writers and journalists, I fell back, naturally, on Shahid's collection *The Country without a Post Office*, only to realize that no one— absolutely no one—was a match for him. Eventually, I ended up using a couplet from Shahid's ghazal 'Of Light' as the epigraph to a section of my novel. Although the political subject matter of the collection was important, it was the aesthetic sensibility, reflected in his language, that made it remarkable. Much later, I read in an interview that Shahid always placed the aesthetic value over the subject matter of his poems.[2] For three years leading up to the publication of my novel, I had used Shahid's works as a lens through which I saw and understood Kashmir. In time, however, the lens itself became the object, which I started looking at from a fresh set of eyes.

I suspect that one of the reasons I fell in love with Shahid was because his poems mapped all the languages, cultures and worlds that I believed I belonged to. Shahid was completely South Asian and completely cosmopolitan at the same time, and in his poems, I could sense the presence of both Ghalib and Eliot, of the West as well as the subcontinent. But as I delved into his work, I discovered that there were more layers than I could have ever imagined.

Shahid was a beneficiary of three cultures—Hindu, Muslim and Western—and at his home, poetry was recited in four languages—English, Urdu, Persian and Kashmiri. Although he wrote in English, his poems, in essence, captured the sensibilities of all these languages and traditions. His father, Agha Ashraf Ali, was an educationist with socialist inclinations and introduced him to the ideas of Mahatma Gandhi, Jawaharlal Nehru and Martin Buber, while his mother, Sufia Agha, a Sunni Muslim from Uttar Pradesh, sang bhajans to him and dressed him as Krishna for Janmashtami. While on the one hand his paternal grandmother, Begum Zafar Ali, was a devout Shia Muslim who taught him about Islam, on the other hand he went to a Catholic school and, throughout his formative years, was fascinated by Christ. I soon realized that Shahid was the sum total of these different cultures and learnt from all of them, that he never viewed them as contradictions but simply as different world views that later coalesced in his poetry.

In his poems, there is not only the presence of these cultures and traditions but also several allusions to the works of other writers and poets. Much like Eliot had done in some of his poems, Shahid weaved into his work the words of other poets, such as Osip Mandelstam, Faiz Ahmad Faiz, Emily Dickinson, John Milton, Rainer Maria Rilke, Paul Celan, Yannis Ritsos, Octavio Paz and C.P. Cavafy—who, for me at the time, were not his precursors but poets who flowed through him. It was almost as if his poems had doors which one could open and enter a different world altogether. 'They [the readers] should be devouring poetry all the time, and some of the pleasure is in recognizing,' Shahid once said in an interview.[3] He was indeed a poet in whose works existed a universe, and in time, the influence of all the poets I discovered through Shahid's poetry shaped my understanding of history, geography and language in numerous ways. At the same time, as I read these poets, my admiration for Shahid grew. Shahid's poems, I realized, were on the same pedestal as the poems of those others, and I came to respect him even more for he was, from my point of view, the centripetal force that bound all of them together for me.

In the summer of 2016, I moved to New Delhi for my master's degree in English literature. It was the city Shahid was born in, in 1949, and where he spent seven years of his life—from 1968 to 1975. In Delhi, I saw Shahid's poetry everywhere—in the

streets that 'light up / with the smiles of beggars'; at Jama Masjid,
I witnessed how the 'minarets camouflage the sunset', how the
prayers rose 'brick by brick'.[4] Although I could trace Shahid's
poems in Delhi and Srinagar, when I started looking for the
poet, there wasn't much, barring a few articles and tributes by his
friends and students, some academic papers on the Internet, and
the introduction to *The Veiled Suite* by his friend and poet Daniel
Hall. Now that I look back, I believe it was in the summer of 2016
that I first thought about writing Shahid's biography.

Although I had already started reading beyond his poetry,
discovering him through his family and friends and writing
about him while I was still at university, in January 2018 I met
Shahid's brother, Agha Iqbal Ali, at the India International
Centre in Delhi to discuss the biography for the first time.
He narrated a trove of stories about their childhood, stories
that had led to poems. I sat and simply listened to all that he
had to say. After a few meetings, in May 2018, I found myself
in Srinagar, at Sufia Nishan (Harmony 3, the house Shahid
had grown up in, was renamed Sufia Nishan after his mother's
demise). The house, beyond the boundary wall, was white, and
the lawn had sparse plantation. Later, I was told that the house
had been ravaged by the floods of 2014 and was rebuilt. It was
a warm and sunny day. On the lawn, Iqbal was instructing the
gardener, who was planting roses. We sat in the shade on the
porch of the house, which overlooked the lawn. I mentioned it
was warmer than I expected it to be, to which Iqbal responded
by reciting Robert Frost's 'Two Tramps in Mud Time' as a
word of caution.

It was there that I met Agha Ashraf Ali for the first time.
Although his reputation preceded him—I had read a dozen essays
about his contribution to education in Kashmir—it was only
after meeting him that I understood why people such as Sheikh
Abdullah, the first 'prime minister' of Jammu and Kashmir, and

notable educationists like Zakir Hussain and Mohammad Mujeeb were impressed by him. Even at ninety-five, he was always reading, always surrounded by books. When Iqbal told him that I was writing a book about Shahid, his face lit up with a smile. I promised him that I would come to Srinagar to give him a copy as soon as it was published. However, that was never meant to be. On 7 August 2020, Agha Ashraf Ali passed away at his home in Rajbagh, leaving an incredible legacy behind him.

I travelled to various cities, from Srinagar and Lucknow to Goa, to meet Shahid's friends and family. After interviewing more than forty people and taking more than a dozen flights, I finally decided that the only place left to scour was the Agha Shahid Ali archives at Hamilton College in Clinton, New York. However, there was a strange turn of events: I was denied a visa by the American embassy. Those were the years of the Trump administration, whose signature issue was immigration policy. In time, I eventually received all the documents that I required, one of which was, funnily enough, an essay by Shahid titled 'Dismantling Some Silences', published in the 1989 spring issue of *Poetry East*, in which he had criticized the United States' immigration policy and asked questions that his father would present rhetorically at dinner parties in Muncie in the 1960s:

Would America give Christ a visa if he were to appear by chance, his robe torn and his hair covered with dust, before a US Consul in Damascus or Khartoum or Baghdad? Christ, after all—my father continued—believed in a just distribution of wealth: he had divided the fish and loaves equally and had kicked the money lenders out of God's house—radical, by many American standards. Our Hoosier guests looked uncomfortable: the question had altered their usual discourse of self-congratulation about the land of the free. They had to admit, to themselves, that Christ would have been denied a visa (perhaps to the

embarrassment of the nations of the world which might then
have convened a special session of the General Assembly in
Geneva?).[5]

Reading his letters, the drafts of his poems and the interviews, I
realized that even though Shahid was constantly negotiating his
identity, he had made it clear that for him, language was the only
homeland. 'First and foremost, I consider myself a poet in the
English language,' he once said in an interview.[6] But with that
came another, perhaps a more important realization—that Shahid
was unlike any other contemporary poet I had come across. At a
time when there are so many attempts to dissolve the person and
the poet, Shahid emerges as an exception.

Shahid had decided to become a poet at the age of nine, and
throughout his life he worked towards achieving this goal. He was
so riveted by his poetic pursuits that he ended up turning into
a manifestation of his art. However, what made Shahid truly
special was that he was always aware of the distinction between his
personal life and his poetic pursuits, and though his personal life
overlapped with his poetic persona, it was in a way that I had never
encountered before. Shahid was indeed what T.S. Eliot called a
'mature' poet, one whose life wasn't more interesting but was, as
opposed to an immature poet, 'a more finely perfected medium in
which special, or very varied, feelings are at liberty to enter into
new combinations', whose personal emotions or the emotions
provoked by an eventful life didn't make him interesting, but his
impersonality, which he achieved by 'surrendering' himself 'wholly
to the work', did.[7]

Shahid was always on the lookout for a phrase or a line that he
could turn into a poem, and so much of his poetry came to him,
as with the mystics of Kashmir and Sufi saints, from dreams and
visions. The writer Amitav Ghosh, his friend, believed that 'in his
determination to be not just a writer of poetry but an embodiment

of his poetic vision, he was, I think, more the heir of Rumi and Kabir than [T.S.] Eliot and [James] Merrill'.[8] Shahid drew a clear distinction between his poetry and his personal life, and yet he put all of himself into his art. This is what makes Shahid's poetry so different, where the more one reads his poems, the more he truly reveals himself to the reader.

* * *

'Darling, I don't want immortality through my works,' Shahid once said, quoting Woody Allen, to his friend and publisher Rukun Advani. 'I want immortality by not dying.'[9] Although his works have attained immortality both in the Indian subcontinent and the West, this biography is my attempt to keep Shahid—or at least his memory—alive, as he had wished.

However, it is an ambitious and an exhaustive task to imagine all aspects of a person's life. Thus, as a biographer, I was forced to make a choice, to single out the aspects of his life that I wanted to explore. Given his status as a globally renowned poet and the fact that there have been no attempts in the past to memorialize his life, I chose to focus on different facets of his personality and concerns which ultimately lead the reader back to his poetry. This interests me more than divulging the details of his private life, which might be the subject for future biographies and is important in its own right.

In this book, I have attempted my best to highlight his relationship with people like the singer Begum Akhtar, the poet James Merrill and the scholar Eqbal Ahmad, as well as to focus on the events of his life that shaped his poetic concerns, which ranged from grief and nostalgia to history, politics and war. Even his wit and humour, which led to the extravagant light verses and, to some extent, contributed to his appeal and magnetism, find a place in this biography.

Arguably, no poet in recent times, at least in the Indian subcontinent, has received as many readers and as much attention after their death as Shahid. In a scenario such as this, I believe that this book serves as a foundation for further research and investigations into various other aspects of his life and work that I might have overlooked. My hope is that this biography will provide answers to some questions that surround Shahid's life and poetry, but more importantly, that it will allow readers to explore the mind of a poet whose verses have become, in recent years, more relevant than ever.

Prologue

Dark Krishna

In a photograph from the early '50s, Shahid is dressed as Krishna. A crown rests on his head, although at the time he was unaware of what it represented or who the 'blue, invisible god' was. The picture was taken at Jamia Millia Islamia in Delhi, when Shahid was barely two years old. A few years later, when they were in Kashmir, his mother dressed him as Krishna on each Janmashtami and took him to the refugee home she ran. In time, his admiration for Krishna grew, and dressing up as the Hindu god turned into a precious memory.

The partition of the Indian subcontinent in August 1947 was an enormous tragedy. As soon as the British Raj came to an end, the subcontinent was divided into India and Pakistan (which would later be subdivided to form a new nation, Bangladesh), and bloodshed followed. Right after the declaration of independence, the largest recorded migration in history took place. Millions of Muslims headed towards East and West Pakistan, while Hindus and Sikhs tried to find their way to India. Although trains full of people left from one side of the border, they only delivered corpses. Myriads never made it across. Thousands were slaughtered, orphaned or widowed overnight. Those who survived turned into refugees. It caused wounds that people on both sides of the border have been tending to ever since. It is estimated that around

75,000 women were raped during this defining moment in South Asian history.[1] Many Hindu and Sikh women who had made it across the border were marooned in an unfamiliar land. While some of them had faced sexual abuse, abduction and rape, others had lost their families to sectarian violence and were left all alone. It was these women that Mridula Sarabhai had set out to help.

Mridula belonged to the illustrious Sarabhai family from Gujarat. They were industrialists and philanthropists who were involved in the freedom struggle and had contributed to various developmental tasks across the nation after Independence. Her father, Ambalal Sarabhai, was the owner of Calico Mills, one of India's oldest mills, while her brother, Vikram Sarabhai, was a famous physicist who co-founded the Indian Space Research Organisation. Although Mridula came from an influential family, she had turned into a prominent figure in Indian politics of her own accord. She was an ardent supporter of Mahatma Gandhi and of the Kashmiri leader Sheikh Abdullah. Gandhi admired her work and vision to the extent that he had once proclaimed: 'If I had a hundred women like Sarabhai, I could launch a revolution in India.'[2] He had, in fact, personally assigned her the task of identifying, relocating and helping women refugees.

It was during a visit to Kashmir in the early '50s that Sarabhai met Sufia Agha, who had just returned to Srinagar from London with a diploma in child development. Sarabhai had come to Kashmir looking for someone to lead the rehabilitation operations at a regional level. She was charmed by Sufia, by her knowledge and understanding of trauma and psychology, as well as by her love for children. Soon after their meeting, Sarabhai urged Sufia to run a state-sponsored refugee home in Srinagar for Hindu and Sikh women refugees in Kashmir. Although Sufia wanted to be a part of this humanitarian task, after giving the matter some thought, she refused. She was the mother of three young children who needed her attention and care. Taking the responsibility of those women, she thought, wouldn't be fair to anyone involved in the equation. However, Sarabhai was adamant for she had witnessed Sufia's magnetism and was moved by her demeanour. She returned, offering to turn a custodian property behind Sufia's house into the centre, so that it would be easy for Sufia to manage both her children and the women. Sarabhai's persuasion proved effective, and Sufia started working at the refugee home.

Sufia was a compassionate person who was mindful of everyone around her. At home, she was attentive and cared about the minutest of details, making sure that everyone felt loved. Agha Iqbal Ali, Shahid's younger brother, stresses that his mother's love wasn't 'a zero-sum game but an infinite pie'.[3] Sufia attended to everybody in a ceremonial manner. In turn, whoever met her was impressed by the warmth and empathy she emanated. It was the same for the women and girls at the refugee home. She interacted with them at a personal level and had a relationship with each of them. Under her watch, the girls were taught skills such as weaving and tailoring, aimed at making them financially independent and allowing them a dignified life once they left the home.

The impact of her work was such that it changed their lives forever. Those women never forgot the help they had received during what would have been the toughest time of their lives. Iqbal remembers how once, years later, in Jammu's Raghunath Bazaar, he and Sufia were stopped by a woman who prostrated herself to touch Sufia's feet. Both the mother and son were baffled. It was only when the woman got up did Sufia realize that she had been at the refugee home years ago.

At the refugee home, there was no compromise on any aspect, be it education, formal training or even something as simple as day-to-day conversations. Sufia had turned it into a large family where the women and girls looked after each other. On all festivals, be it Hindu, Muslim, Sikh or Christian, there were celebrations and everyone participated. It was a secular environment where all religions were given equal importance. However, since most women were Hindu, Janmashtami was an important festival there. Thus, each year, Sufia dressed Shahid as Krishna and took him for the celebration. He was the centre of attention there, surrounded by women who sang bhajans dedicated to Krishna. According to Iqbal, the young boy dressed as Krishna came as a new hope for the women who lived there, who had lost all faith in god.

Shahid remembered this small tradition forever, and Krishna became an important figure in his life. A few years later, when he realized who Krishna was, Shahid went through what Iqbal calls his 'Krishna phase'. He not only dressed as Krishna but also ran around the house with an idol, asking his parents to help him build a temple. Decades later, he recalled this precious moment in an elegy for his mother:

> . . . and I, one festival, crowned Krishna by you, Kashmir
> listening to my flute. You never let the gods die.[4]

Illustration 1: Shahid with his sister Hena Ahmad (*left*)
at Jamia Millia Islamia, New Delhi, c. 1950.

ONE

The Season of Plains

Sufia, who permanently moved to Kashmir with Ashraf in the '50s, spoke of the monsoon with nostalgia. The monsoon season never crossed the Himalayas to reach the valley of Kashmir. When Shahid was a young boy, Sufia would tell him about the monsoon with immense joy. It was a season when 'lovers couldn't bear separation', when Krishna's flute was 'heard on the shores of the Jamuna'.[1]

Sufia was born and raised in Rudauli, a town barely fifty kilometres from Faizabad in the erstwhile United Provinces of Agra and Oudh (present-day Uttar Pradesh). The town was famous for its Sufi saints, and Sufia had also grown up listening to bhajans dedicated to Krishna. Although after her marriage she accepted Kashmir as her home, she had retained the culture of her land and took great pride in it. She was one of the few women in Kashmir who wore a sari—a garment traditionally worn in Uttar Pradesh but quite uncommon in Kashmir at the time. Years later, Shahid remembered his mother's love for her birthplace and wrote, 'She, a Muslim from Lucknow, had Hindu folk traditions in her bones.'[2] In 'The Season of Plains', he recalled his mother's love for Krishna, Lucknow and the monsoon:

In Kashmir, where the year
has four, clear seasons, my mother
spoke of her childhood

in the plains of Lucknow, and
of that season in itself,
the monsoon, when Krishna's

flute is heard on the shores
of the Jamuna.[3]

Sufia belonged to a family that could trace its lineage to Sufi saints and mystics from Uttar Pradesh. Her name, too, meant someone who was Sufi-like. Shahid often said that his mother had the 'grandeur of a Sufi',[4] although this impression was derived from her values and not just the name.

Uttar Pradesh, the land of the nawabs, has cradled the Ganga–Jamuni *tehzeeb*—the syncretic Hindu–Muslim culture which upholds religious harmony—for centuries. After the British conquest of Awadh in 1856, the kingdom's last independent ruler, Wajid Ali Shah, was exiled to Calcutta. Following the annexation, people from the region resisted English influence. They viewed the British as oppressors, and believed that preserving the Awadhi traditions and culture would keep their identity alive. Even during Sufia's formative years in the early twentieth century, people from the United Provinces had managed to retain various elements of their culture. They were known for their finesse, etiquette and civility throughout the subcontinent. These shades of elegance and sophistication that were so deeply ingrained in the fabric of the land had manifested in Sufia as well. According to Hena Ahmad, Shahid's elder sister, Sufia's style and the way she conducted herself around people set her apart from other women in Kashmir.

Although Awadh had resisted English ways of life, by the early twentieth century children from privileged families had started attending convent schools, owing to the lack of good schools in the region. Sufia, too, joined the Crosthwaite Girls

College in Allahabad. There, she lived with her maternal uncle Syed Siraj-ul-Hasan, who was the president of the regional branch of the Indian National Congress. Sufia completed her schooling, and in 1946, during her FA (the initial degree offered before Bachelor of Arts), a marriage proposal arrived for her.

A young Kashmiri called Ashraf, a teacher at Jamia Millia Islamia in New Delhi, had asked for her hand. The proposal had come through Dr Zakir Hussain, who was the chancellor of the university and later became the President of India. Sufia decided to meet Ashraf. The meeting took place in Lucknow. The twenty-four-year-old Ashraf was a cultured man and was among the Jamia educationists who were revered in the northern part of the subcontinent. Soon after the meeting, their marriage was decided, even though there were sectarian differences—Sufia was a Sunni and Ashraf was a Shia Muslim.

In October 1946, the wedding took place in Lucknow, and Sufia moved to New Delhi, starting a new life in the capital. Although Ashraf was a Kashmiri, he had decided to stay in Delhi. He considered Jamia his home, where he was among educationists and intellectuals like Hussain and Mohammad Mujeeb. After their marriage, Sufia too began teaching young boys at Jamia—which, in the '40s, also had a school—and weaved herself into the fabric of the community of educationists. Although the young couple were aware of the ongoing political changes, they had no clue as to what the future had in store for them.

In less than a year, India declared independence from the British Raj, and horrors of enormous proportion followed right after. Their lives were disrupted in a way they had never expected. Sufia had imagined that her life with Ashraf would be in Delhi. However, in the years that followed, she settled in Srinagar. Surrounded by the Pir Panjal range, far away from the dry plains, she would listen to thumris and songs of devotion, longing for the monsoon, 'When the clouds gather / for that blue invisible God . . .'[5]

TWO

Jamia

Ashraf was born to Agha Zafar Ali and Begum Zafar Ali in Srinagar while it was still the capital of the princely state of Jammu and Kashmir. He was raised in the picturesque city that had mushroomed around the Dal Lake and the snaky Jhelum River, surrounded by the Pir Panjal range on one side and the Himalayas on the other. However, the beauty didn't count for much to Ashraf for he was an 'unwanted child'.[1]

When Begum Zafar was pregnant for the third time, she was expecting a daughter. But to her dismay, it was another son. Ashraf's paternal grandfather had married a young woman named Begum Qamar-u-Nisa after the death of his first wife. The young bride was childless, and to please her, Ashraf was sent to live with his grandparents as soon as he turned two. Although it left a deep mark on Ashraf, in time it turned into a blessing, for he was raised by one of the most illustrious men in Kashmir: Khan Bahadur Aga Syed Hussain.

Aga Syed Hussain, born in August 1876, was the grandson of Hakim Bakir, who was the chief physician of Maharaja Ranbir Singh of Jammu and Kashmir. In her autobiography, *Meray Shab-o-Roz*, Begum Zafar Ali wrote that at the time of Aga Syed's birth, royal astrologers had claimed that had he been born into a Hindu household, he would have been an avatar of Lord Vishnu.

But since he was born in a Muslim family, he would grow up to be a man of power and influence. In time, the royal astrologers' claim came true. In 1894, Aga Syed Hussain travelled to Rawalpindi on a tonga to sit for the matriculation examination at the University of Punjab, becoming the first matriculate from Kashmir.

Although Maharaja Pratap Singh was biased against the Muslim population of Kashmir—it is said that his aversion towards the Muslims was so extreme that he didn't like to even look at a Muslim until noon[2]—he couldn't ignore Aga Syed's acumen and knowledge. Upon his return, Maharaja Pratap Singh offered him a place in his court because of his command over English. Later, Aga Syed held various administrative positions across the state. He finds mention in Muhammad Din Fauq's *Tareekh-e-Aqwam-e-Kashmir* (History of the People of Kashmir) as Kashmir's first English-speaking Muslim.

For long, Muslims in Kashmir had remained uninterested in modern means of education and were thus on the back foot when it came to administrative positions. Even at the dawn of the twentieth century, they feared that Christian missionary schools and foreign education would turn them into apostates and remained faithful to madrasas and *maktabs*.[3] However, by the mid-twentieth century, there was a paradigm shift in how education was imparted in Kashmir. With the gradual establishment of various schools and colleges, a small segment of the Muslim youth population started receiving modern education, although state records from those years show that the majority of Muslim youths barely attended school.[4] But because of Aga Syed, education was an integral part of one's upbringing, and as soon as Ashraf turned four, he was sent to the Christian Mission School at Fateh Kadal.

Not only did Aga Syed leave an impact on the young boy, he also trained him in ways that transformed his life forever. The turbaned man raised Ashraf to compete at the highest level. Under his watch, Ashraf experienced much more than his brothers Nasir and Shaukat had. In 1928, when Maharaja Pratap Singh established the High Court of Judicature for Jammu and Kashmir, Aga Syed was appointed the home and judicial minister. Ashraf, who was only a boy at the time, travelled with Aga Syed whenever he visited the Jammu durbar or major cities like Lahore and Karachi. Recalling his formative years, Ashraf once said: 'His [Aga Syed's] influence on me throughout the first twelve years of my life was the basic factor that shaped my life. It was not only because of the type of man he was but because of the kind of selfless love he showered on me and the way he educated me in those years.'5 Growing up around him, Ashraf understood that Aga Syed had established himself as an important figure through his skills and qualifications. Ashraf soon came to the conclusion that a person's stature was linked to their education. Even his mother, Begum Zafar, was revered in the Valley for she was Kashmir's first female matriculate. Fortunately for Ashraf, his natural inclination for learning was inspired by his grandfather.

Ashraf returned home after spending twelve years with his grandfather and joined Sri Pratap College in Srinagar for a bachelor's degree. Although the time he spent in college was fruitful, it was largely banal, barring one moment during the third year that changed his life.

In 1938, N. Gopalaswami Ayyangar, the then prime minister of Jammu and Kashmir, invited Zakir Hussain to Sri Pratap College as the keynote speaker at the All-India Muhammadan Educational Conference. Hussain was the chancellor of a fairly new but promising university in Delhi called Jamia Millia Islamia. A part of the Indian freedom movement and an ardent follower of Gandhian philosophy, he was known for his oration and demeanour. His speech that day delineated various ways in which education could be improved. In the audience was the sixteen-year-old Ashraf, who was impressed by Hussain's speech. Much later, recalling the events of the day, he said: 'For the first time, I felt that I was in the presence of what you would call greatness. His manner of speech, eloquence—it just bowled me clean.'[6]

Hussain had practically changed the way education was viewed in the subcontinent, especially among Muslims. After graduating from Aligarh Muslim University (AMU) in 1918, he, along with other educationists, established the National Muslim University in Aligarh at the age of twenty-three. In 1922, he left for Germany for a PhD in economics at Friedrich Wilhelm University in Berlin, returning to India three years later with Muhammad Mujeeb and Syed Abid Hussain—two Oxford students he had met in Berlin. The triumvirate shared a passion for education and together took Jamia to new heights. By the late '30s , he (along with Mujeeb and Abid Hussain) had become the face of modern Indian Muslim thought. Ashraf was charmed by his intellect. In Hussain, he saw a mirror image of his grandfather, who had shaped his world view; and thus, Ashraf decided to follow Hussain to Jamia. Decades later, remembering this phase of his life, Ashraf would quip, 'That was how my troubles began in life.'[7]

Ashraf spoke to Hussain after the Sri Pratap College lecture and asked if he could come to Jamia to learn from him. Hussain was delighted but told Ashraf that he should get a master's degree before coming to Jamia; he suggested that Ashraf go to AMU. In any case, it was a natural choice for Ashraf. 'In those days, it was an unsaid rule in Kashmir that Muslims went to AMU while the Pandits attended Banaras Hindu University,' Iqbal recalls.

Ashraf applied to AMU for a degree in history and was accepted. On arriving at the university, he wrote a letter to Hussain saying he was on his way to Jamia. In three days, he received a reply: 'If you decide to make a present of your life to your people, please make sure that you are making a worthy present.'⁸ Ashraf took the advice seriously, and at AMU he showed signs of brilliance. He was taught by learned people like Mohammad Habib (Mujeeb's brother), who was one of India's finest historians. At AMU, Ashraf stood first and earned a Morrison Medal, eventually moving to Jamia as he had planned.

At Jamia, he was mentored by Hussain and Mujeeb, whose influence shaped his personality in ways he had never imagined. He was introduced to the visions of leaders like Gandhi, Jawaharlal Nehru and Maulana Abdul Kalam Azad, who were closely associated with Jamia. These leaders and figures from the Indian independence struggle had always supported Jamia. When Jamia was in dire straits financially in the mid-'20s, Gandhi had famously stated: 'If you're facing a financial crunch, I am ready to carry a begging bowl and go door to door. But Jamia must continue.'⁹ Apart from Indian thinkers and leaders, Ashraf was also exposed to European thinkers and philosophers like Martin Buber and Karl Marx, whose ideas instilled in him a socialist ethos that called for equality, justice and individual freedom. These values stayed with him and shaped the outlook of his children. Not only are they present in Shahid's poems but were also integral to his demeanour and the way he imagined the world.

Once Ashraf became a part of this community of educationists, he gave up his feudal lifestyle, adopted a life of khadi and imagined that he would spend the rest of his life in Delhi. When Hussain and Mujeeb realized that Ashraf had decided to stay on at Jamia, they suggested he marry a girl from Uttar Pradesh. Ashraf agreed and the search for a suitable match began. By October 1946, Sufia and Ashraf were married and settled in Delhi. However, less than a year later, their lives changed with the sudden end of the colonial rule.

Illustration 2: Agha Ashraf Ali, Sufia Agha, Shahid and Hena at
Jamia Millia Islamia, New Delhi, c. 1950.

Ashraf understood all that was going to happen, for he was around people who played a vital role in Indian politics at the time. While on the one hand, there was a camp of leaders which included Gandhi, Nehru, Azad as well as Hussain and Mujeeb, another group had already started forming. In 1930, the poet Allama Iqbal had delivered a presidential address at the annual meeting of the Muslim League, where he planted the seeds for the two-nation theory.[10] After Iqbal's death in 1938, Muhammad Ali Jinnah took this view forward and advocated the formation of a separate state for Muslims called Pakistan.

This view was completely different from Ashraf's understanding of history. Jamia was a product of both the Khilafat as well as the non-cooperation movements, and the imagination of Hussain and Mujeeb was different from that of Jinnah. Although leaders like Gandhi and Azad had opposed Partition, the much-awaited moment of freedom was marked by the great divide. The bloodshed that followed further broke the two new nations at the moment of their inception, and India and Pakistan were left licking their wounds caused by the violence. The effects of Partition have lingered on ever since. Not only did it lead to mass migration and several wars over seven decades, but it also spelt doom for Ashraf's homeland, Kashmir, turning it into a geopolitical point of contention.

Ashraf, like Hussain and Mujeeb, believed in a unified nation where both Muslims and Hindus could coexist peacefully, and these ideas informed his children's understanding of South Asia's biggest political event. Although Shahid grew up in the '50s, when the fires of Partition had been stubbed out, it was still a reality for him as much as it is for anyone in the subcontinent today. Shahid only had second-hand memories of the event that had survived as a fracture in the collective memory of the subcontinent. Naturally, Shahid wrote about the bloody wounds the event left in its wake:

> The two-nation theory is dead
> But the old don't forget
>
> In this city of refugees,
> Trains move like ghosts.
> The old don't forget.
>
> My friend's grandfather,
> Hoarder of regrets,
> cautions: 'Those Muslim butchers:
> Be Careful, they stab you in the back.
> I lost my beloved Lahore.'
>
> My friend and I are rather simple:
> We never saw the continent divide.[11]

When at the stroke of midnight on 15 August 1947 Nehru declared independence from the British with his 'Tryst with Destiny' speech, Ashraf and Sufia were in Jammu, and they returned to Delhi shortly after. In the capital city of the newly formed nation, a massive rebuilding project had begun, which included infrastructural, constitutional and institutional reforms. Soon, Jamia became an important centre for the education of India's Muslim youths under the watch of Hussain. His quality and leadership didn't go unnoticed, and Indian leaders coerced him to take up the chancellorship of AMU, which was already a prominent institution and required the attention of a seasoned person. When Hussain said yes in 1948, it came as a setback for the twenty-six-year-old Ashraf, who was about to become a father. Sufia was pregnant with their first child. On 7 February 1948, she gave birth to their daughter, Hena, in Lucknow. By that time, Hussain had left Jamia and was on his way to AMU.

Following Hussain's exit, Ashraf decided to move to Kashmir to become an educationist there. When Ashraf expressed his desire to go to Srinagar, Hussain was pleased and wrote to Sheikh Abdullah, referring Ashraf for a position in the state's education department. Abdullah had risen to power in the '30s as an anti-establishment leader and had caught the attention of Nehru. In May 1946, Abdullah started the Quit Kashmir movement against the Dogra regime of Maharaja Hari Singh, for which he was imprisoned. However, once Hari Singh acceded to India on 26 October 1947, Abdullah was appointed the prime minister of the state.

By 1948, turmoil had already started in the Valley. Pakistan and India had started fighting for Kashmir, turning it into a conflict zone, as Kashmiris demanded independence. Abdullah was aware of Ashraf and his family, and though he believed Ashraf was capable, he wanted him to explore European schooling systems before taking up the position. In a letter to Ashraf, Abdullah wrote: 'You must go around Europe, study their schooling system and once you're back, we'll find a position for you.'[12] He informed Ashraf that although they didn't have the money to send him to Europe, the government would give him a loan. This marked an important shift in Ashraf's life. He had planned to spend his whole life in Delhi, but now, he was not only moving to Kashmir but also getting an opportunity to study in Europe. It was around this time that Sufia was expecting another child. As dawn approached on 4 February 1949, she gave birth to a son in a nursing home in Okhla. They named him Shahid.

Ashraf left for London a year after Shahid's birth, and later that year, Sufia joined him there with their two children. While Ashraf worked on an academic diploma in comparative education and educational organization and administration, Sufia enrolled for a diploma in child development. There weren't many South Asian families in London in the '50s. According to Iqbal, when the family stepped out on the streets, 'it was a sight'.[13]

By the time Shahid had learnt to crawl, he started to garner a lot of attention. Once, on a train to Devonshire, the two-year-old Shahid had slipped from his mother's gaze, crawled under the table and smacked an English lord who was busy reading the newspaper. The lord, flabbergasted, could do nothing and went back to reading his paper, while Ashraf and Sufia tried to control their laughter. In time, it turned into a cherished memory of their time in England, one that was narrated to Shahid when he grew up.

Illustration 3: Shahid and Hena in Devonshire, England, c. 1951.

Ashraf completed his diploma in 1951, after which he went to several European countries with Sufia, leaving the children in London with a caretaker. They went to what was then East Berlin on a boat called the MS *Batory* to attend the 3rd World Youth Festival, and then to Denmark and Sweden. Eventually, via France, they returned to London, from where they left for India. One week after their arrival in New Delhi, on 11 December 1952, Sufia gave birth to Iqbal. When the family of five arrived in Kashmir, Ashraf was appointed as an officer on special duty under Sheikh Abdullah. Within a year, owing to his experience and knowledge, he was appointed the inspector of schools at the age of twenty-eight. Ashraf made use of all that he had learnt at Jamia and in Europe, working towards the education of Kashmiri youths for the next five decades, setting an example for his children to emulate.

THREE

Harmony 3

As soon as the family arrived in Kashmir in 1952, the first floor of their house, Harmony 3—an art deco-style house based on Austrian architect Karl Heinz's design—was turned into a nursery for the children. To make it look like a space conducive to children, an art teacher from Teacher's College in Srinagar was commissioned to paint pictures of giraffes, elephants and other animals on the walls. Another section on the first floor was turned into a study, with a huge blackboard and a play area for the siblings that was fitted with a slide. Iqbal remembers that 'there was no compromise when it came to things that were essential, like education'.[1] The adjective that Shahid used most when describing his childhood was 'rich' and its variants. Although he was raised in a well-to-do family of influence, what he truly meant by 'rich' was to refer to the value systems that had shaped him. When the time came to send them to school, Ashraf, because of his socialist inclinations, decided that Shahid would go to a government school.

Ashraf was a commanding figure who achieved everything he set out to do. 'I began my administrative career, fearless, turning everything upside down and inside out under Sheikh Abdullah's total protection and guidance, and I never looked back. Everyone was angry with me. The entire bureaucracy hated me . . . Whatever was the right rule, I implemented it without any fear or favour. The first order I issued on 1 April 1953 was about the transfer of Sheikh sahib's nephew.'[2] Ashraf set up new schools all around Kashmir and reformed the old ones using European standards. For him, it wasn't just an infrastructural job but one that included the task of changing the mindset of people. Coming from a Marxist background, he set out, with education as his tool, to uplift all the neglected sections of society, including women (it was an uncommon practice in those days to send girls to school).

Even at home, Ashraf was a figure who tried to inculcate certain values in his family. While he ensured that his children received all the exposure they needed, he sent Shahid to a government school. However, that lasted only for a few months. Seeing the lackadaisical as well as irresponsible attitude of the teachers, Sufia put her foot down and pulled Shahid out of the school. Eventually, he was enrolled in Presentation Convent, an Irish Catholic school that was a stone's throw from Harmony 3.

Shahid's first exposure to the world, like most people, was through his family. The value systems he had inherited were his father's socio-political beliefs and his mother's compassion and finesse. Although Ashraf's ambition was the dominant trait in Shahid's character, the side that emitted empathy came from Sufia. Vidur Wazir, whom Shahid became friends with at Presentation Convent at the age of four, recalls that Shahid grew up in a 'very open and progressive environment' and attributes it to the beliefs and ideas of his mother. 'He was fortunate to have a mother like that—she was fantastic! Psychologically, she knew how to work with children.'[3]

At home, Shahid was exposed to different cultures, religions and languages. When he became aware of Krishna, he told his parents that he wanted to build a Hindu temple in his room, and they helped him place the idol. When he demanded that he wanted to build a Catholic chapel with a picture of Jesus, Sufia and Ashraf bought a statue and said to him, 'Go ahead, build your temple.' Decades later, Shahid recounted that 'there was never a hint of any kind of parochialism in the home' and that 'it was a wonderful atmosphere of possibilities of self-expression'.[4]

Throughout the '50s, Sufia and Ashraf held mushairas at Harmony 3 which were attended by family and friends. During the mushairas, Iqbal, Hena and Shahid were sent upstairs. When they snuck their way back to the ground floor and peeked through the door, they would hear the adults repeating, 'Wah wah!' Blissfully unaware of what was happening, they would mimic the elders and giggle. With time, Shahid and his siblings developed an understanding of poetry. When he was only a young boy, he had absorbed a lot of poems through his father. While on the one hand Ashraf read Russian writers like Fyodor Dostoevsky, on the other hand he also recited the verses of Persian and Urdu poets—one of whom was Faiz Ahmad Faiz. In one of his essays, Shahid remembers the presence of Faiz during his childhood: 'I must have then begun to internalize Faiz, because I often found myself repeating these, as well as other lines, to myself. Without having any clear sense of what the lines meant, I still somehow felt the words, felt them through their sounds, through the rhythms of my father's voice.'[5]

Shahid's youngest sister, Sameetah (b. 1965), remembers how her father sang the songs of K.L. Saigal, which, according to her, 'evoked a whole era'.[6] As a teenager, Shahid revisited these songs and wrote a poem about the singer. While he inherited his admiration for Faiz, Mirza Ghalib, Saigal and other ghazal singers from his father, his mother introduced him to singers like Rasoolan Bai and Begum Akhtar, and to Awadhi culture. At Harmony 3, poetry was recited in four languages: Kashmiri, Urdu, Persian and English. His grandmother, Begum Zafar, recited verses by Kashmiri poets like Zinda Kaul, Mahjoor and Habba Khatoon as well as by Urdu poets like Mir Taqi Mir. What surprised him most was his grandmother quoting lines from the works of John Milton, Thomas Hardy, John Keats and Shakespeare.

In the sixth grade, Shahid was admitted to Burn Hall School, which had reopened in Srinagar after Partition in 1956. At Burn Hall, Shahid was an atypical backbencher; he was smart yet mischievous. Wazir recalls that they had a teacher called Ms Pant 'who Shahid used to find very funny. Throughout her class we would keep giggling—it's the one thing I clearly remember. She'd say something and we'd look at each other and just burst into laughter.'[7] At the time it was only a class of a dozen students, including the children of Indian Air Force officials and a few German kids whose parents were working as architects and engineers for the construction of the Jawahar Tunnel, which connects Jammu to Kashmir.

At Burn Hall, Shahid was introduced to rock and roll and other genres of Western music that were fairly new in the subcontinent at the time and had started making their way into Indian movies. 'There were these dance moves that everyone wanted to copy,' Iqbal remembers. 'So the question was, "How were you going to do that?" And then, they'd end up going to the teachers to learn those dance moves.'[8] In his teens, Shahid listened to Edvard Grieg, Elvis Presley, the Beatles and Chopin. His mother read Greek myths to him. Much later, he wrote, 'The Hepburns, both Katharine and Audrey, were part of my imaginative life as were Madhubala, Meena Kumari and Suchitra Sen.'[9] At home, there was an amalgamation of all these languages, cultures and music which shaped his understanding of the world and, later, informed his poetry in various ways. Speaking about these 'historical forces' that had formed him, he once said:

The historical forces in my case are that I come from Kashmir, and I'm a product of Hindu, Muslim, and Western influences. I write in English—and I have always written in English. It could have been otherwise, too. My parents, my interest in music, my interest in poetry, Indian classical music, Western classical music, Western popular music, all these things since my childhood have informed my being. The thing that makes them historically interesting is that the combination is unusual. Because one can say that of anybody—a combination of forces has shaped each one of us. What makes it particularly interesting, I suppose, is that I do it all in English, so I am able to do certain things in English for the first time.[10]

At Burn Hall, along with Wazir and another friend named Pavan Sahgal, Shahid had formed a small trio, an exclusive group called 'The Silent Three'. The name came from a British comic strip from the '50s by Horace Boyten and Stewart Pride, about three schoolgirls at a boarding school who band together as a secret society against the tyranny of the head prefect. Together, Shahid, Wazir and Sahgal would practise plays and skits that would be performed at school and would spend time listening to Western music on tapes. 'From *Henry VIII* to *Red Riding Hood*, we performed everything, and tea would be served later. It was a wonderful environment, full of culture and life,' Wazir remembers.[11] After the plays, their friends from school were invited to Shahid's place, where they had snacks and desserts from Ahdoos, which was, at the time, a reputed patisserie whose proprietor had been sent to Calcutta by the Maharaja to learn French baking.

Shahid stood out at school in academics and also took an interest in what the teachers had to offer. At Presentation Convent, Shahid's teachers were Anglo–Indians from Bombay who wore Western dresses and had a modern outlook on life. While the other children loitered around, Shahid and Wazir sat with the teachers in their rooms discussing Western music and listening to the songs that had just come out. At home, Shahid, Hena, Iqbal and Wazir listened to All India Radio programmes such as

A Date With You and *For the Forces*, which played Western music.
Wazir remembers that Shahid had a small notebook with lyrics in
them so that he could remember the words to the songs to impress
the teachers.

Although Sufia, Ashraf and Begum Zafar inculcated certain
values at home and Shahid learnt much at school, there were
other people, too, who had a massive impact on Shahid during his
formative years. The family visited Mohammed Mujeeb whenever
they went to Delhi, and in time Shahid started looking up to him.
When Shahid and Hena were young, Ashraf chastised them for
reading Erle Stanley Gardner's series of Perry Mason mystery
books. Then, one winter, they visited Mujeeb at his house at Jamia,
which Iqbal remembers as 'a beautiful stately home in art deco style
designed by Karl Heinz with a spiral staircase and a floor-to-ceiling
library'.[12] There, Shahid and Hena started going through the books
only to discover an entire collection of Perry Mason books. 'So,
from then onwards,' Iqbal recalls, 'whenever Daddy would say
anything about those books, their (Shahid and Hena's) response
would be: "But Mujeeb Sahib reads Perry Mason." For both of
them, it was almost as if Mujeeb had knighted Stanley Gardner.'[13]

In January 1968, Iqbal and Shahid visited Rashtrapati Bhavan
in Delhi with Ashraf to meet President Zakir Hussain. As soon
as they arrived at the presidential palace, the aide-de-camp
escorted Ashraf to Hussain's office, while the family was taken
to the President's family quarters. Soon, however, the aide-de-
camp came and said that Hussain wanted to meet the boys, who
were then taken to his office. Meeting and speaking with Hussain
immensely influenced both the boys.

Ashraf was of the view that 'Shahid had access to the finest
minds available in India—it was such a privilege'.[14] When these
people visited Harmony 3, the siblings were always around and
spoke with them about various things, like poetry, music and
history. As a teenager, Shahid would often persuade Mujeeb to

accompany him to theatres for movies like *Pakeezah*. During the film, Shahid, along with Mujeeb, laughed when the actress said, '*Ek har raat, teen baje, ek rail gaadi apni patriyon se utar kar, mere dil se guzarti hai aur mujhe ek paigham de jaati hai* (Each night, when the clock strikes three, a train leaves its rails, crosses my heart and delivers a message),' because he recognized the contrived nature of the dialogue. Even during the climax of *Mughal-e-Azam*, when the crowd in the film starts to shout 'Zindabad! Zindabad!', Shahid burst into laughter.

These small incidents show why a figure like Mujeeb was also interested in spending time with Shahid. His magnetism was irresistible, and he attracted almost everyone towards himself. It was people like Mujeeb, and later Begum Akhtar and James Merrill, who had a certain understanding of the world, a certain finesse about them, who got to Shahid. What Shahid was exposed to as a child was the best, and when he saw the best minds of the nation in front of him, he naturally, like his siblings, wanted to emulate them. While he was fortunate to have these influential people around him during his formative years, there were also some initiatives that he took himself.

During the harsh winters of Kashmir, the family would either move to Jammu—the winter capital of the state—or New Delhi. In 1960, while driving through the capital of India, they drove by Teen Murti Bhavan, the Indian prime minister's residence in those days. The eleven-year-old Shahid was curious about who lived there. 'Chacha Nehru,' Ashraf replied. Jawaharlal Nehru, the first prime minister of India, was quite fond of children and came to be known as Chacha Nehru. Fascinated by the image of the man who lived in that building, Shahid decided to write a letter to Nehru, which Ashraf posted to Teen Murti Bhavan. 'That was the end of that,' Iqbal remembers. 'But a few days later, an official car, with the tricolour fluttering, arrives at our house. And the messenger presents an envelope for Shahid.'[15]

Nehru had invited Shahid, along with his family, to Teen Murti Bhavan. They went there on 18 February 1960. 'The morning he had invited us,' Shahid recalled in an interview, 'I was so sleepy that I told Mummy, "Oh, I don't want to go."'[16] But once he was there, along with Iqbal, Hena and his mother, they were ushered past the people sitting on the carpet and sofas in the hall into the main drawing room of the residence. They were the only people present there. Once Nehru came through the hallway, Shahid got up to garland him. But Nehru ended up garlanding Shahid instead.

Illustration 4: Shahid (*right*) and Iqbal with Prime Minister Jawaharlal Nehru at his residence, Teen Murti Bhavan, in New Delhi, 18 February 1960.

In a photograph from the prime minister's residence, Nehru's hands rest on the backs of Shahid's and Iqbal's necks. Another picture shows Shahid in Nehru's arms with a gleam on his face as the Indian prime minister smiles at the young boy. Iqbal remembers that Shahid asked Nehru, 'What can I bring you from Kashmir?' to which Nehru replied: 'What more can I want when I have two intelligent boys like you? What more can I want?'[17]

This memory remained with Shahid forever, and he shared Nehru's secular and progressive vision. However, by the time Shahid met him, Nehru's tryst with Kashmir and his relationship with Sheikh Abdullah had taken a sour turn, and Kashmir's destiny had been altered forever.

FOUR

The Awakening

Veronica is said to have lived in Jerusalem when Christ was alive. Although her story failed to make its way into the Bible, the first written account about her appears in *The Avenging of the Saviour* (circa eighth century CE). According to legend, Veronica stopped Christ when he was on his way to Calvary from Jerusalem for the crucifixion. As she wiped Christ's face with her veil, an imprint of his face miraculously appeared on her kerchief. Soon, a cloth with Christ's face became a venerated object in Rome.

The concept resurfaced as Europe woke up to the Renaissance. Dante referred to it in *Paradiso*, and it became a popular subject—painters such as the Master of the Legend of St Ursula, Peter Paul Rubens and Bernardo Strozzi painted St Veronica's legend and her cloth. One of the renditions is *St Veronica's Handkerchief*, an 1874 lithograph by Gabriel Cornelius Max. The Austrian painter only painted the face, leaving out St Veronica or the moment when the face appeared on her veil. It is not only one of the most beautiful depictions of the Veil of Veronica but also one of the most magical. Fourteen colours were used in the sepia painting to get an effect: if one looks at the eyes long enough, they seem to open up, if only for a moment.

A replica of the lithograph adorned the walls at Harmony 3 when Shahid was growing up—it was a gift from Zakir Hussain, who had bought it in Berlin. One can imagine the young Shahid asking his father about it and what it symbolized. Shahid attended a Catholic school, and there was, as is the case with most Catholic schools, a typical fascination with Christ and Christianity around him. Shahid had formed a childlike interpretation of his own, and Christ's story had cemented its position in his mind. He often went to the nuns asking for rosaries and holy pictures. Thus, when Shahid wrote his first poem at the age of nine, it was about Christ. The poem was titled 'The Man'.

Ashraf would hear Shahid recite poems with joy. When Shahid showed him his first poem, he was delighted with his son's achievement. Ashraf rewarded him by gifting him a leather-bound journal for his poems, with an inscription that read: 'Spontaneous self-expression must now grow into studied attempts at conciseness and discipline.'[1] Although the act of picking up a pen and expressing himself in verse was important to Shahid, his father's approval caused an awakening in him. What had been a pastime turned into an active pursuit within a few years.

Years later, Shahid admitted that though his first one was not a 'bad poem', the ones he wrote after that were 'horrible, horrible poems'.[2] Even though he was becoming more and more aware of the world in his late teens, Shahid developed a naive sense of poetry and decided that he wanted to become a poet. In a letter to Shahid on 25 January 1979, two weeks before his thirtieth birthday, Sufia had written: 'Your ambition at nine of becoming a poet and appearing to understand and appreciate Greek and Russian literature—all have given you a very rich experience of life.'[3]

In 1953, Sheikh Abdullah was imprisoned by the Indian government following the Kashmir conspiracy case, and Bakshi Ghulam Mohammad was appointed the prime minister of the state. As soon as Abdullah was jailed, Ashraf resigned from the position of inspector of education. 'It [Sheikh Abdullah's arrest] changed everything,' Ashraf said in an interview. 'The entire bureaucracy hated me and before they had the pleasure of throwing me out, I wrote to Bakshi sahib, "Since I don't see eye to eye with your director of education, I beg to be removed from the present post."'4 After his resignation, Ashraf became the principal of Teacher's College of Education in Srinagar. He stayed in Kashmir for some more years, but by the late '50s, he decided to apply for a Fulbright scholarship.

In 1960, Ashraf left for America to visit teachers' training colleges at Columbia University, University of California (UCLA), the State University of New York at New Paltz and Ball State Teachers Training College. While he was at Ball State in Muncie, Indiana, the faculty he met was impressed by his acumen and suggested that he stay there and work on his PhD. Ashraf agreed to do that, and in May 1961, Sufia, along with their three children, joined him in America. In time, the college turned into Ball State University, and Ashraf became the first person to receive a PhD from the institute.

To get to America, Sufia and the children had boarded a ship to the Tilbury Docks in the UK, spent a week in London and then taken the *Queen Mary* from Southampton to America. Shahid, who was then in the eighth grade, was admitted to Burris Laboratory School, which was located on campus. There, he was taught by people who already had their PhDs, and thus, naturally, were far more experienced than his previous teachers and left an impact on the young Shahid. In his application to Ball State University for a master's degree in 1968, Shahid wrote that he was deeply impressed by Dr Anthony Tovatt, his English teacher at Burris Lab. It was there, he said, that he realized he could 'best find the means to express myself through literature' and since then had 'wanted to teach literature at a university'.

Illustration 5: Shahid, dressed as a scarecrow, receiving the first prize
at a fancy-dress competition on the SS *Arcadia* on the
Mediterranean, 1961.

Theirs was the only non-American family at Ball State. It was there
that Shahid started understanding poetry and literature, and was

exposed to new Western music, which he took back with him to
Kashmir. Although Shahid, Iqbal and Hena's command over English
was much better than the natives', the time spent at Burris Lab made
him realize 'many aspects of life which young people cannot normally
[comprehend]'. In his university application, he wrote:

> If I have to single out one experience, it would be my three-year
> stay in America. It altered my whole life and what I am today,
> I am because of my stay in America. One is bound to be lonely
> and depressed in an alien society. One feels uprooted. But in the
> long run, one feels wiser and grateful. What is more important,
> one can see one's own country in a cleaner and more objective
> perspective.[5]

What he meant by that last line was that in America, there was a
general awareness of the idea of home. Far away from Kashmir,
for the first time, Shahid started acknowledging the beauty of his
own culture. 'When we moved to America, Daddy had a very rare
tape of Begum Akhtar singing Faiz's "Mujhse Pehli Si Mohabbat
Mere Mehboob Na Maang", which he took with him to Ball State,'
Iqbal recalls. 'One day, Bhaiya and Hena were playing the cassette
and listening to Begum Akhtar. I started saying wah-wah and
giggling, but both of them asked me to hush. They were older—
Bhaiya and Paru [Shahid's sister Hena] must've been twelve or
thirteen—and had started understanding and reacting to Begum
Akhtar's music and the verses of Faiz.'[6]

The American literary critic Bruce King, writing about
Shahid's time at Burris, said that he was 'well integrated in
the school, was encouraged to write by a teacher and is still
remembered with affection by former class mates and teachers.
When he returned to Muncie for a poetry reading in 1990 at Ball
State University, he also read at Burris School and parties were
given in his honour.'[7]

Illustration 6: (*Left to right*) Hena, Ashraf, Shahid, Sufia and Iqbal when Ashraf received the first PhD at Ball State Teachers College, Muncie, Indiana, 1964.

Once he returned to Kashmir, something had changed in his bones. Shahid had started responding to music and art from the Indian subcontinent. Far away from home, he had developed a newfound appreciation for subcontinental music—he didn't take it for granted any more. In time, he realized much more about his identity and the roots from which he had sprouted.

Once the family returned to Kashmir in November 1964, Shahid became more aware of the painting of Hakim Naqi Ali, his 'grandfather's grandfather / son of Ali', in the living room of his house. It was here that he understood that there was a benchmark set by his ancestors and that he was a product of those historical forces. Not only did this shape his attitude, it also helped him feel the presence of 'generations of Snowmen' riding on his back.

Shahid's family could trace their history to the Persian Qizilbash clan, who were mercenaries in the armies of Nader Shah and the Safavid Shahs. The family's history in Kashmir went back to the early nineteenth century, when their ancestor Raheem Qizilbash Aala Qadr moved to the Valley. Although Raheem had the blood of warriors flowing in his veins, he was a merchant who procured rugs, ashrafis, fur skins and emeralds, rubies and other gemstones from Kandahar and sold them in Kashmir. After two generations, following the First Anglo–Afghan War (1839–42), the Qizilbash were persecuted in Kandahar for siding with the British. As the doors to their homeland were shut, trade stopped, and Raheem's grandchildren, Muhammad Bakir and Muhammad Taqi, were born into poverty. The family had spent all the wealth and even sold their family heirlooms in order to survive. Their father, who had perhaps seen this coming, had trained them in Yunani medicine.

In 1872, Maharaja Ranbir Singh of Jammu and Kashmir was on a *parindah*—a large boat rowed by twenty-four people—on Manasbal Lake. As he was crossing the Khanqah-e-Sokhta, the Maharaja complained of a severe stomach ache. When his condition started deteriorating—he had started screaming because of the pain—the royal physician was summoned. He tried everything, all potions and salts, but failed to alleviate the Maharaja's pain. The Maharaja soon fainted, at which point, his men ran towards the closest village in search of another hakim. The villagers asked them to knock on Bakir's door, who they believed was the most competent hakim in the vicinity. Bakir ran to help the Maharaja, blissfully unaware of how his life was going to change.

The initial suspicion was that the Maharaja had been poisoned, but when Bakir examined him, it turned out to be a much simpler condition. He gave him some potions and salts, and in no time the Maharaja broke wind—as legend has it, it was a long and thunderous fart which moved the clouds, clearing the sky—and was relieved of the pain. As a reward, Agha Bakir was granted a *jagir* of 1000 *kanals* (a unit of area used in northern India, equivalent to one-eighth of an acre) in various parts around the Valley, bestowed with robes of honour and appointed the chief physician to the Maharaja. Decades later, Shahid narrated the story and quipped: 'So you see, the fortunes of my family were founded on a fart.'[8] Although he joked about it, this weight of history had a massive impact on Shahid, and he recounted all of it in the first section of *The Half-Inch Himalayas*, in which he writes of his ancestor, 'a man of Himalayan snow':[9]

My ancestor, a man
of Himalayan snow,
came to Kashmir from Samarkand,
carrying a bag
of whale bones:
heirlooms from sea funerals.
His skeleton
carved from glaciers, his breath
arctic,
he froze women in his embrace.

Perhaps Shahid was conscious that he was 'the last snowman', for he was the eldest grandson of Begum Zafar Ali. Even if that wasn't the case, there was in him definitely an awareness about his birthplace and history which eventually found its way into his poems. Shahid was born into a Shia Muslim family and was very much aware of that. Begum Zafar, Shahid's grandmother, finds mention in his poems more than once. He grew up watching her pray, and she often recited the Koran to him and played a vital role in his childhood.

Begum Zafar was, like her father Aga Syed, the first female matriculate from Kashmir and an advocate of women's rights and education. She worked as headmistress at different schools in the Valley and, later in life, was appointed secretary of the All India Women's Conference. In 1987, she was awarded the Padma Shri, the fourth-highest civilian honour in India, for her work.

But when unrest began in Kashmir in the early '90s, she publicly returned the award, condemning the human rights violations.

Although Begum Zafar was a modern woman, her beliefs were deeply rooted in Islam. It was through her that Shahid understood the Muslim world. Later in life, he would refer to Husayn ibn Ali's martyrdom and Muharram processions in his poems, as well as to small things such as waking up at dawn to pray. Still, when it came to religion, Shahid's outlook was very different from his grandmother's. For him, religion was a 'system of feeling' and had more to do with feelings than beliefs.[10] Shahid had once said that his greatest problem with some religious people was that they offered him a 'scientific' theory of religion: that God existed and had a plan and so on. However, he found it to be 'maddening'.[11] His perception of religion was, in some ways, quite similar to that of Ghalib and Faiz, who brought religious elements and Muslim iconography to their poetry and turned them into metaphors, but without confining themselves in the sphere of religion. Shahid's poetry, from the very beginning, had humanist values rather than nationalist or religious implications. He touches upon this in 'Note Autobiographical—2':

> I asked Grandma: Is God a Muslim?
> 'Kafir! you're no good,' she said.
>
> No one taught me the Koran
> My father mouthed Freud and Marx
> something about recognizing necessity
> and India bleeding for our smooth skins.
> Mother had long since discarded the veil.
> We ate pork secretly.[12]

At Harmony 3, there was an amalgamation of various ideas and beliefs, and Shahid absorbed all of them. His father's socialist thought and the ideas of German thinkers had a massive impact on Shahid's understanding of religion. Sufia brought in a mix of Sunni Muslim and Hindu traditions from Lucknow. His grandmother was a devout Shia. At school, he became acquainted with Christianity and the West. And growing up in Kashmir, he came to acknowledge the vast history of Kashmiri Shaivism. However, Shahid never viewed these differences as contradictions and learnt from all of them. He belonged to everyone and no one at the same time. All these elements, which stemmed from his experiences, are present in his poems. As in 'Prayer Rug'[13], where he weaves his father's socialist views into the fabric of the Muslim tradition he was witness to:

> this rug
> part of Grandma's dowry
> folded
>
> so the Devil's shadow
> would not desecrate
> Mecca scarlet-woven
>
> with minarets of gold
> but then the sunset
> call to prayer
>
> the servants
> their straw mats unrolled
> praying or in the garden
>
> in summer on grass
> the children wanting
> the prayers to end

In 1965, the youngest of the four siblings, Sameetah, was born. The same year Shahid turned sixteen, finished his schooling and joined Sri Pratap College for his bachelor's degree in arts (with philosophy, history and English as the primary subjects). Each morning, he crossed the Jhelum on a shikara, climbed the stairs that led to the Bund and from there, crossed Lloyd's Bank, Ahdoos and Preco Studio, and walked past Mir Pan House and Regal Cinema to reach the campus.

He spent much time either at the India Coffee House drinking coffee or at the Kashmir Book House shuffling through their collection. On some evenings, his friends would come over for casual visits, while on other days, Shahid and his siblings hosted parties for them. The Kashmiri society was conservative in the 1960s. Intermingling between the sexes was not considered natural for the most part. But at the parties at Harmony 3, there would be regular 'mixed' gatherings. Shahid invited all his friends. There was music—Western and Indian—and dancing. 'He was a brilliant dancer,' recalls Wazir. 'There was no one like him at those parties—everyone wanted to dance with Shahid.'[14] Kamla Kapur, who met Shahid after both of them had graduated from high school, wrote about Shahid's brilliant dance moves:

> I don't remember who invited my sister and me, or was it just me, to a 'mixed' dance party. The only thing I remember about that party so long ago was Shahid. I don't remember being introduced to him. Memory sifts things down to the essentials, and sometimes even that threatens to go, now, at almost 71. But O, I do remember dancing with him! I don't remember dancing like that ever again, except with my husband, Payson, in our own living room, when we first met. Payson and my dance was free form, while my dancing with Shahid was the old, traditional way, the guy guiding, the woman following. But in that dance no one was guiding or following anybody.

We were moving together as one body. The dance was us and
we were the dance. We talked and chatted through most of it.
It must have been an intimate discussion. Shahid was gay in the
old, traditional sense—bright, cheerful, lively.[15]

By that time, Shahid was not only aware of what he wanted to
do and become but was also mindful of the standard that had
to be achieved. He didn't just want to be a poet, he wanted to
become a good poet. But he still had a long way to go, and along
the way, he would come across great poets who would influence
him in ways he couldn't have imagined. One of them was T.S.
Eliot. Perhaps the only contribution of SP College to Shahid's
personality and poetry was this introduction he was given here
to Eliot's work, which he recounted in 'Introducing': 'A Ph.D.
from Leeds / mentioned discipline, casually / brought the waste-
land.'[16] Later, Shahid's doctoral theses at the Pennsylvania State
University would be about Eliot: *L'Entre Deux Guerres: T.S. Eliot
as Editor*.

The American poet remained a massive influence on Shahid
and his poetry. His presence in Shahid's verses is palpable in *Bone
Sculpture* and *In Memory of Begum Akhtar*, especially in the poem
'Cremation', which Shahid wrote after his friend Vidur Wazir's
mother's death, as well as in 'Introducing', where he turns Eliot's
'mixing memory and desire' to 'mixing blood with mud, memory
with memory'. Shahid's friend Saleem Kidwai remembers that
when he was teaching at Delhi University, Shahid 'spoke about
Eliot all the time, incessantly. I knew nothing about Eliot, and he
would go on and on.'[17]

Eliot's verses, everything from 'The Love Song of J. Alfred
Prufrock' to *Four Quartets*, had a profound impact on how Shahid
approached the idea of poetry. With time, his voice gained Eliot's
scepticism, loneliness and his denial of the present. Shahid read
Eliot and his poems meticulously, breaking them down to the

last feather to see what he had done and how he'd managed to do it. This was how Shahid came to understand certain aspects of poetry. During those years, the poems Shahid was writing were too close to his lived experiences. It was primarily by his reading of Eliot that he understood how to distance himself from his personal experiences and approach them in a 'mature' manner.

In 1972, Sumi Sridharan, who taught at IP College in Delhi University, wrote a review of *Bone Sculpture* and noted that '[t]he weakness of Shahid's writing is the abstractness of some of the experience and the echoes from Eliot that mar even a good poem like "Bones"'.[18] Although he still had much to learn, Eliot's influence did wonders for Shahid, helping him grasp the niceties of language and also the importance of tradition.

It was at this point, during his graduation, that Shahid first read Eliot's essay 'Tradition and the Individual Talent'. In it, Eliot redefines the idea of tradition and stresses its importance in poetry, before stating that poetry ought to be impersonal. He classifies poets into mature and immature poets, and states that for a mature poet, 'poetry isn't a turning loose of emotion, but an escape from emotion; it is not the expression of personality, but an escape from personality'.[19]

What Eliot meant by impersonal wasn't that poetry shouldn't come from personal experiences, but that a mature poet should separate the self, the one who suffers, from the mind of the poet that creates. These ideas practically changed Shahid's outlook. His poems became much more informed and complex than before, and he started taking cues from his intellectual concerns rather than from his personal life.

However, by the mid-'70s, Shahid had started becoming disillusioned with Eliot's politics. When he became aware of Eliot's anti-Semitism, he grouped him with other fascists like Ezra Pound and Wyndham Lewis, and started calling him a 'horrible poet'.[20] But he soon started separating his politics from his aesthetics and announced that, 'We must enlarge our sympathies, historicize simplicities and complexities, and learn even from—dare I say it?—from fascists'.[21] At the same time, Shahid started reading Eliot more seriously and concluded that even poems like 'The Love Song of J. Alfred Prufrock', which had influenced Shahid as a teenager, were deeply personal and could not 'transcend the intensity of emotions'.[22] In a paper written in 1978 critiquing the poem, Shahid wrote about Eliot's approach and questioned if it 'revealed a poet who had tradition in his bones':

> [T]radition has to be obtained by great labour. But does 'The Love Song' reveal a poet who has the tradition of Europe in his bones? Eliot, we cannot help suspecting (and believing), manages to use tradition; he is aware of it. But he is not traditional. Thus 'The Love Song' remains an isolated act of genius. It fails, besides artistically, on two basic grounds: it is not in a tradition, and it is not impersonal. There is hardly any separation between the man who suffered and the mind that created.[23]

Reading Eliot's poetry helped Shahid gain a lot of insights during the first decade of his career. Through Eliot, Shahid learnt how to incorporate in poems allusions to the works of other poets and realized the importance of sound in a poem. This knowledge stayed with him for the rest of his poetic career, for he understood, through Eliot's approach, that the artistic genius in poetry emerged only when it was impersonal. 'Tradition' and 'impersonality'— these two words remained with him for his entire life and have, since his death, shed much light on his works. When Shahid was pursuing his bachelor's degree at SP College, Eliot was the poet he looked up to. But when he moved to New Delhi for his master's degree in English literature, his reading of Eliot improved further, and he also discovered other poets whose works would stay with him forever.

In 1968, for the first time in the history of Kashmir University, the topper of the batch was from an arts course. A professor of philosophy at SP College had met Ashraf at a dinner and mentioned that there was an exam paper he had recently assessed to which he couldn't resist giving 140 marks out of 150. He said that the boy's thinking was impeccable. Ashraf was impressed. What the professor and Ashraf didn't know at the time was that the boy was Shahid—the answer sheets didn't have any names, only roll numbers.[24]

Soon after the declaration of the results, Shahid and Iqbal, who had finished his schooling, applied to St Stephen's College in New Delhi. However, when the admission result was declared, neither Shahid nor Iqbal, who had applied for physics honours, found their names in the admission list. Shahid rushed to the principal's office and asked for an explanation as to why he wasn't selected. 'I have a first class first degree,' he said to the principal, to which the latter responded: 'So why don't you go somewhere where you can keep your first class first degree?'[25]

Aghast, Shahid and Iqbal went to meet P.N. Dhar at the Institute of Economic Growth in Delhi. Dhar was a family friend and an eminent economist who later became principal secretary to the Indian prime minister Indira Gandhi, before taking up the position of assistant secretary general, Research and Policy Analysis, at the United Nations in New York. He was married to Sheila Dhar, the famous Indian author and Kirana gharana singer. As soon as Dhar became aware of the situation, he called his close associate K.N. Raj, the vice chancellor of Delhi University. Dhar said to Raj that there were two kids from Kashmir, the sons of eminent educationist Agha Ashraf Ali, and that they had been denied admission even though they had met the merit requirements.

The next day, both the brothers were informed that they had been admitted to the college. However, at this point, Sheila Dhar, who had graduated top of her class from Hindu College in 1950, intervened and said, 'But why do you want to go to Stephen's now? There's no point. You should go to Hindu College.'[26] Shahid and Iqbal agreed and joined Hindu College, right across the street from St Stephen's.

FIVE

In Streets Calligraphed with Blood

In the summer of 1968, Shahid ventured out of the familiar for the first time when he moved to New Delhi. As is the case with anyone who moves out of their home for the first time, it was the beginning of a new phase of life for him. He was living on his own in the college hostel, trying new things, like cooking, that he had never done in Kashmir. In Delhi, he created his own world, one that was different from the one in which he had grown up. This new world was full of possibilities. The city would, at the end, teach him how to manoeuvre through life. As a teenager in Delhi, he witnessed the monsoon that his mother would speak of with passion and nostalgia. In an interview, he recalled the brilliance of the season in the capital of India:

> We have rain in Kashmir, which sometimes leads to floods, but it does not have quite the same feeling as rain in Delhi has. When I went to Delhi for the first time in summer, in July, and I saw these rains, I [saw] a very romantic season and could see why you would want to be in the arms of your lover.[1]

Later, when he became a professor in the early '70s, Shahid started living in a *barsati* (a room on the top of a house with a bathroom) in what is now known as the North Campus area of Delhi. Since there were limited rooms in the hostels, students had taken over areas around the university, such as Model Town, Vijay Nagar, Kingsway Camp and Outram Lines in the northern part of New Delhi. 'I used to live in 83 Tagore Park, not very far from Shahid,' Rupendra Guha Majumdar, Shahid's friend during his seven years in New Delhi, said about their time as students at Delhi University. 'There were lots of dhabas and tea stalls to group around and eat at. That's where we met often and talked endlessly about poetry, and about how to teach literature to our students. There was this Mama's dhaba, we used to call its owner Mama [Uncle]. He was so Falstaffian, you know—big paunch, dark fellow, always laughing and smiling. Those discussions at the dhaba were so animated. I remember he [Shahid] used to hang around with his friends. Saleem was there, Sunil was there.'[2]

Illustration 7: Shahid in Batkote, Kashmir, 1973.

In Delhi, Shahid discovered a world of opportunities that was not so easily accessible to him in Srinagar, a world that offered him not only exposure to poets and poetry, but also simple pleasures of life, like films and music. Shahid recited his poems at various colleges in Delhi University. In the first two years of his arrival in the city, he had come to be known as an aspiring poet. His recitations were marked by humour and wit, and he was loved by almost everyone. In turn, the 'Kashmiri Moslem' boy fell in love with the city where he was born.

It was at a poetry reading at Daulat Ram College that Shahid met Saleem Kidwai for the first time. Saleem remembers that he came with a friend, Aman Nath, who was also a poet. Shahid read 'Cremation' as the opening poem. 'For almost all the poetry readings,' Saleem remembers, 'Shahid began with that poem. It was a crowd-pleaser meant to hook everyone in, a clever, very clever poem[3] . . . meant for *taalis* [applause].'[4] Saleem was a student of history at Jamia and two batches junior to Shahid. Although the first time they met was almost three years after Shahid had moved to Delhi, Saleem was one of the few people from the city Shahid remained friends with for a long time.

Shahid was always, especially in those days, in search of a phrase or an utterance, anything that had the potential of becoming a poem. In an interview with Akhil Katyal, Saleem narrated a story: 'There was no electricity. We were smoking near the window, very late at night. There was only one cigarette left so we were sharing it. Suddenly Shahid, this is what he used to do so often, came up with a line: "We light a common cigarette, we smoke a common destiny." He always came up with stuff like this, gems, and as soon as he had said it, he wanted to write it, he was like *"light jalao, yeh to poem ban jayegi"* [switch on the light, this will surely become a poem] and he started looking for pen and paper in the dark, with no light.'[5]

Right after his graduation, Shahid was offered a job at Delhi University. Three years of exposure to poetry and literature, as well as his stature as a young and emerging poet, cemented his position in the Delhi literary circles. He wasn't only a good poet but also a creative teacher. He once asked a class to write an essay on a novel they had recently read or liked. One student responded by asking, '*Lady Chatterley's Lover?*' Shahid said, 'Okay, the book begins, "Ours is essentially a tragic age, so we refuse to take it tragically." Write on the relevance of this statement to our century.'[6] The student came running to Shahid after the class, asking if he could write on something else.

Shahid had, by this time, become familiar with much more, besides his growing obsession with Eliot. 'He would often recite [Oscar] Wilde, especially "The Ballad of Reading Gaol",' Saleem remembers.[7] Shahid introduced Saleem to Lawrence Durrell's *The Alexandria Quartet*, which became one of his favourite books; and Saleem, in his turn, discussed E.H. Carr's *What is History?* with Shahid, from which Shahid would later quote a line in his elegy for Begum Akhtar: '. . . you cannot cross-examine the dead.' 'When he presented books, he always had a funny way of inscribing them. He was extra conscious that it doesn't suggest extra form of closeness [to the person the copy belonged to],' Saleem said, laughing. 'It was always a joke.'[8] Sejal Shah, Shahid's student at Hamilton College, recalls how in her copy of *The Country without a Post Office*, Shahid had taken up the entire front page for the inscription:

For Sejal—Shah of Shahs!—
So royal, so princely—
So regal—so she
Who couldn't go to Spain
Is going to Italy!
Ah![9]

By the late '60s, Indian parallel cinema was becoming known in the world and 'new wave' film-makers, such as Mani Kaul and Kumar

Shahani, had released their debut films. But it was also the era when the aesthetics of parallel cinema had started seeping into popular cinema. Even though Shahid had watched Guru Dutt's *Sahib Bibi Aur Ghulam* numerous times in Jammu with Wazir, he went for the screening of the film whenever it was playing in Delhi and even Ghaziabad in Uttar Pradesh, which was then considerably farther away than it seems today. Shahid would take a bus to watch the film with Saleem, coming back in the evening. Shahid picked up moments from films such as *Sahib Bibi Aur Ghulam*, *Pakeezah* and the iconic *Mughal-e-Azam*. Aman Nath remembers that Shahid absolutely loved Meena Kumari and Madhubala, and that he would never miss a film which featured the former.

Shahid responded to serious movies and admired films like Satyajit Ray's *Pather Panchali*, which he had watched in his pre-teens. One film that stayed with him was *Jhanak Jhanak Payal Baaje*, which he had watched as a young boy. The movie, featuring the Indian dancer Gopi Krishna as the lead, has numerous dance performances, which deeply influenced Shahid. So much so that Shahid went for Bharatanatyam and sitar classes after watching the movie. Much later, in his poem 'Flight from Houston in January', he evoked a moment from the film that had stayed with him in his thirties. Lines from a song—'*Badal naiyya hai bijali patavaar / ham tum chal den duniya ke par*'—remained in his memory as an unforgettable image:

> If clouds were boats,
> one would row them
>
> with rods of lightning,
> across the world.[10]

The songs, especially from the more serious films which touched their subject rather gently and poignantly, stayed with Shahid for a long time. In those days, because there wasn't any other way to listen to music, Saleem, Shahid and Aman would go to Rhythm Corner, a small shop run by Manga Advani and his wife near Scindia House in Delhi, where they had listening booths. Shahid would spend all his free time there listening to records, because a single record would cost about Rs 40, which was, at the time, very expensive. On Shahid's birthday, Saleem gifted him a harmonium, although in hindsight, Saleem says that it was a mistake because Shahid wouldn't stop playing the harmonium and singing along with it. 'He was quite a *dramebaaz*,' Saleem recalls. 'He wanted to be the centre of attention at every gathering—and he was, because he really had a charming personality.'[11]

In Delhi, Shahid also became aware of the city's Mughal and colonial history, and was impressed by its architecture. In the early '60s, the Mexican poet Octavio Paz had visited New Delhi and had been charmed by its architecture. He wrote numerous poems about the city and about all that he had witnessed here. He found Delhi's 'aesthetic equivalent' in 'novels, not in architecture', and to him, wandering the city was 'like passing through the pages of Victor Hugo, Walter Scott, or Alexandre Dumas'.[12] Paz's gaze, wherever he went, was directed inwards. For him, all the experiences, including the splendour of the Mughal architecture that attracted him, were revelatory and enlightening in one way or the other. In his book *In Light of India*, he called Delhi's architecture 'an assemblage of images more than buildings'.[13] It was quite the same for Shahid who, after nineteen years, had returned to the city of his birth. He was a student at Delhi University, which wasn't too far from Old Delhi or what was once known as Shahjahanabad, the walled city of Delhi constructed by Shah Jahan—the emperor who 'knew the depth of stones, / how they turn smooth rubbed on a heart. / And then? Imprisoned / with no consoling ghosts . . .'[14]

The tomb of Amir Khusro at Hazrat Nizamuddin in Delhi was a place that had attracted Paz. In 'The Tomb of Amir Khusro', he wrote: 'Amir Khusru, parrot or mockingbird: / the two halves of each moment, muddy sorrow, voice of light. / Syllables, wandering fires, vagabond architectures.'[15] The tomb attracted Shahid as well when he visited the dargah in Delhi almost a decade later: 'I come here to sing Khusro's songs. / I burn to the end of the lit essence . . . / The muezzin interrupts the dawn, calls / the faithful to the prayer with a monster-cry: / We walk through the streets calligraphed with blood.'[16]

In Delhi, Shahid found poetry at each turn. In an interview with *First City* in 1991, he said: 'For me the lanes of Delhi, particularly the ones leading to and from the Jama Masjid, hold a dazzling value. When I used to go to Kareem restaurant or was having *nihari* or kulfi on the steps of Jama Masjid, I used to imagine that I was living in the days of Ghalib.' Unlike Paz, who as an outsider in Delhi could only adore the architecture, Shahid also saw history in the city. Although he had been exposed to the historical forces that had shaped Kashmir, it was in Delhi that he discovered, for the first time, history in brick walls, minarets and on the streets. In 'The Walled City: Seven Poems on Delhi', he wrote about Jama Masjid:

> Imagine: Once there was nothing here.
> Now look how minarets camouflage the sunset.
> Do you hear the call to prayer?
> It leaves me unwinding scrolls of legend
> till I reach the first brick they brought here.
> How the prayers rose, brick by brick?[17]

Shahid's poetic concerns were largely a constant for most of his life, and are palpable in these early poems. His engagement with history, which he deals with as both an insider and outsider, reflects his tenderness and the experience of a poet who belongs to multiple worlds and none at the same time. For the next three decades, he wrote about loss and the memory of loss, the burden of history and injustices of all kinds. The seeds of these poetic concerns were sown during his childhood, mostly at home. However, they were nourished in Delhi, by the city's air and its history, which Shahid couldn't ignore.

In the poems from *Bone Sculpture* and *In Memory of Begum Akhtar*, Shahid emerges as a poet who feels deeply about South Asian culture as well as politics. Both the collections are influenced by Delhi and reflect an understanding of history. From a very young age, he was aware of the historical movements, the revolutions and leaders who had shaped the world he lived in. In time, he established his position as a poet of witness with the publication of his poem 'After Seeing Kozintsev's *King Lear* in Delhi', which talks about the last Mughal emperor Bahadur Shah Zafar. In the poem, Shahid makes a conscious choice as he turns from King Lear and looks at Zafar, turning away from fiction towards fact, from the stories of the colonizers to the histories of the colonized. This turn marks an important moment in Shahid's poetry, and it is from here that his poems and sensibility come to be defined by a certain post-colonial outlook, where he sheds light on those whom history had ignored:

I think of Zafar, poet and Emperor,
being led through this street
by British soldiers, his feet in chains,
to watch his sons hanged.

In exile he wrote:
'Unfortunate Zafar
spent half his life in hope,
the other half waiting.
He begs for two yards of Delhi for burial.'

He was exiled to Burma, buried in Rangoon.[18]

In the late '60s, when Shahid joined Hindu College, the syllabus was still under a colonial shadow and predominantly included English writers like John Milton, Shakespeare, Thomas Hardy and the Romantic poets. Although he had read all their works and admired most of them, Shahid's language was very different from the poets that were taught to him. Shahid once said that he was often aware that the music of his language was different, that he was able to bring certain flavours to English poetry in India for the first time, which he believed was a result of the combination of Hindu, Muslim and Western cultures in him, and the fact that he had a 'natural and profound inwardness with them'.[19]

His use of these cultures was not exotic—unlike, say, Eliot importing the word 'shantih' in 'The Waste Land'. Shahid felt them in three languages and didn't have to 'hunt' for subjects. In an essay written much later, he reflected on English poetry in India and said that Satyajit Ray had accomplished what he had because Ray was using a specifically Indian idiom for the first time on celluloid. 'I can use the Indian landscape, and the subcontinent's myths and legends and history from within, and I can do so for the first time in what might seem like a new idiom, a new language—subcontinental English.'[20]

Salman Rushdie's case was similar. Ray, Rushdie (as well as Shahid when it came to English subcontinental poetry) had an abundance of history, tradition and what seemed like an endless river of subjects that they could explore. Shahid had, in fact, acknowledged that if the novel had done it, poetry couldn't be far behind. Little did he know that along with poets like Arun Kolatkar and A.K. Ramanujan, he would become a proponent of English writing in the Indian subcontinent, a poet who had tradition and the flavour of the soil in his bones. In an essay written much later, he reflected on how the English language was changing in the subcontinent:

The colonizers left fifty years ago, and subcontinental writers, particularly poets, can breathe greater confidence into Indian English (as Walt Whitman did into American English) not only because they belong to what, with qualifications, is the international-ism of the English language (in this context, note the awarding of the Nobel Prize to Patrick White, Wole Soyinka, Nadine Gordimer, and Derek Walcott) but because, by re-creating the language, by infusing into it all the traditions and forms at their command, they can make subcontinentals feel that they do not have to seek approval for any idiosyncrasy in syntax and grammar from the queens, Victoria or Elizabeth (the second, of course). As a matter of fact, for all kinds of reasons, it is gratifying to give an insult to the English language.[21]

By the '60s and '70s, some young Indian English poets had started emerging on the literary scene, much of which had to do with Purushottama Lal, the founder of Writers' Workshop, Calcutta. The publishing house started by Lal, which operated out of the library of his residence in Calcutta, had turned into a platform for publishing Indian writing in English. It published the first works of such poets as Nissim Ezekiel, Vikram Seth, Ruskin Bond and A.K. Ramanujan. Lal also published Shahid's first two collections of poetry, *Bone Sculpture* and *In Memory of Begum Akhtar*.

Yet, in the '90s, Shahid wrote in an essay that the 'Indo–English scene' during those decades was 'thoroughly empty and corrupt' and that 'in some quarters' it continued to remain the same, singling out Lal's publishing house, which he said had been functioning as a near vanity press.

In his essay 'Indian Poetry in English', Shahid wrote, 'Educated Indians generally speak three languages, write in two, and dream in one—English.'[22] Although they were written in English at a time when the chutnification, or what he called the biriyanization, of the language hadn't taken place, Shahid's poems were indeed very Indian in nature and in terms of the subjects they dealt with. The English language came to him naturally, while his ideas were deeply rooted in the culture of the subcontinent. Shahid's English wasn't the Queen's 'propah' English but a product of the biriyanization of the language. Although as a poet he was slowly learning, poems like 'Bones', 'Introducing', 'The Walled City' and others not only marked the beginning of a poetic career but also a poetic style that was steeped in a sense of loss, language and the history of the subcontinent. When at last, in the late '60s, he met Begum Akhtar, his appreciation for the traditions of the subcontinent grew and his poetry changed in unimaginable ways.

SIX

Akhtari

In Delhi, Shahid and Saleem never missed the concerts of the well-known singer Begum Akhtar. In a Doordarshan recording of Begum Akhtar singing Faiz Ahmad Faiz's 'Aaye Kuch Abr Kuch Sharaab Aaye', they are sitting in the front row, smiling, as she sings the ghazal, each sentence followed by a *wah-wah*. At one point, she looks at both of them and smiles. Such moments were etched in Shahid's memory, and he would, for the rest of his life, recall them with great passion. 'We were her *chamchas* who would follow her around everywhere,' Saleem remembers. 'Shahid loved her. He loved to be with her, around her—he was always so fascinated by her presence.'[1]

In the late '60s, Saleem moved to Delhi for his master's degree at Jamia. One day, he went to listen to a concert at Sapru House, one of the most famous auditoriums in Delhi. Begum Akhtar (née Akhtari Bai Faizabadi) was performing. As soon as he saw her, Saleem realized that Begum Akhtar had visited his house numerous times. Her family lived in the same neighbourhood as theirs, and she had come with her mother to meet Saleem's grandfather, who was a lawyer. Although Saleem and Akhtari had met a few times, he had never paid attention to her, for he didn't know who she was. When he came back to Lucknow for his vacations, he told his father about Begum Akhtar and said that he had fallen in love with her voice.

One day, when Begum Akhtar came to his house, Saleem's father mentioned that Saleem had attended her concert in Delhi, to which she replied: *'Aap humse milne kyun nahi aate? Hum Dilli aa rahe hain, aap milne aana* (Why don't you come see me? I'm coming to Delhi again, come meet me).'[2] Thereafter, each time Begum Akhtar came to Delhi, Saleem would go to see her even if it was a performance for a small gathering at somebody's place. 'When Shahid realized that I knew Begum Akhtar, that was it,' Saleem recalls. 'There was no looking back then.'[3]

Akhtari was born in Faizabad in Uttar Pradesh in 1914, not very far from Rudauli, Sufia's hometown. 'Subhanallah!' the revered Indian classical singer Gauhar Jaan had exclaimed when she heard a young Akhtari singing one of Amir Khusro's compositions at her school. 'I would love to train her. If she gets the right training, one day she would be known as Mallika-e-Ghazal [the Queen of Ghazals],' she said.[4] Akhtari's mother, Mushtari, took Gauhar Jaan's words seriously, and they moved to Gaya in Bihar, where Akhtari started receiving formal education in classical music under Ustad Imadat Khan and Ustad Ghulam Mohammad Khan. In 1923, they moved back to Faizabad, where she continued her training under Ustad Ata Mohammad Khan from the Patiala gharana, before moving to Calcutta with her mother and guru.

Akhtari's childhood was marked by tragedy, and she carried its burden throughout her life. Her father, a lawyer, had abandoned the family when she was only a child; Mushtari raised her all by herself. The grief-stricken voice that captivated an entire generation was a result of unspoken sorrows. An incident that scarred her for life was when, after a mehfil, Akhtari was raped by one of the rajas of Bihar. Mushtari rushed her back to Lucknow, where she gave birth to a daughter. To protect Akhtari from social stigma, Mushtari announced that the child was hers. The girl was raised as Akhtari's sister, and Akhtari took this secret to the grave.[5]

Although Akhtari hid her pain with a smile, she expressed all of it through her music and her anguished voice.

With time, Akhtari Bai became a well-known singer, famous for her renditions of ghazals and thumris. In 1934, she performed for the first time at a concert organized by Sarojini Naidu for the victims of the Nepal–Bihar earthquake. Naidu later confessed to Akhtari, 'I just came to light the lamp, but couldn't leave after listening to you.'[6] As years passed, she became one of the most sought-after performers in the region and soon, the 'talkies' approached her to act and sing in films such as *Ek Din Ka Badshah*, *Nal Damayanti* and *Roti*. Later in life, she would play the role of a tawaif in Satyajit Ray's *Jalsaghar*. However, all this ended in the mid-'40s when Akhtari Bai became Akhtar Abbasi.

In 1945, she married Ishtiaq Ahmad Abbasi, a barrister from Lucknow, entering the 'respectable' sphere of marriage. After the wedding, she came to be known as Akhtari Abbasi or Begum Abbasi, and although she entered the upper-crust society of Lucknow through this marriage, it came with a price. As a married woman in a patriarchal society, she had to give up singing and live up to the title of 'Begum'. 'As a Begum she could host musical gatherings in her home, but even in privacy relatives, servants, friends, must never hear her be what she had been before,' Regula Burckhardt Qureshi wrote in 'In Search of Begum Akhtar: Patriarchy, Poetry, and Twentieth-Century Indian Music'. 'Personal habits, too, were constricted in a home which was controlled by her strict elder sister-in-law; smoking, for instance, was deemed improper for a lady and had to be confined to the bedroom.'[7]

In 1950, her mother Mushtari, Akhtari's only companion, passed away, and Akhtari sank into acute depression. It is said that when all else failed, Abbasi, with whom she had shared a passion for music and poetry before marriage, allowed her to sing again, for it seemed like the only remedy. However, there was a proviso: she couldn't perform in Lucknow.

In 1951, she performed at Shankar Lal Festival in New Delhi after a seven-year gap, where her name was, for the first time, announced as Begum Akhtar. Although she didn't perform in Lucknow, where she was still known as Begum Abbasi, Begum Akhtar turned into a household name across the subcontinent. Shahid had heard Begum Akhtar ever since he was a young boy and had for long associated her with Faiz. Naturally, her presence during those years played an important part in his life.

Iqbal remembers the first time she came to Harmony 3: 'One fine day, sometime in April 1969—I remember it was raining that day—there was a phone call.'[8] To their surprise, it was Begum Akhtar. In Delhi, Shahid had told her that he would be in Kashmir and had given her their phone number. Begum Akhtar said that she had a flight and wanted Shahid to drive her to the airport. He invited her to Harmony 3 before the flight, and soon, she was there. She got along well with the family, especially Sufia, for both of them were from the same region.

When the time came, Shahid and Iqbal took her to the airport, where she was informed that the flight was cancelled. Shahid invited her to stay at Harmony 3, and she happily agreed. As they headed back, she realized she had run out of cigarettes. 'Both of us drove her in our Fiat to Amira Kadal to buy Capstans,' Iqbal recalls. 'She only smoked Capstan cigarettes, and I remember that she gave me a Ronson lighter, which was very exclusive back them.'[9] As time passed, it turned into one of Shahid's most cherished memories, one that he would recall time and again. From then on, whenever Begum Akhtar came to Kashmir for a concert, she would stay at Harmony 3.

Another time she came to Kashmir was for a performance hosted by the governor. She called Shahid and asked him to pick her up from the airport. When she landed, she found that the governor had sent an official vehicle for her. But Begum Akhtar refused to travel in it. She turned to Shahid and Iqbal and announced, '*Hum toh apne bachchon ke saaath jayenge* [I will go with my kids].' Once the governor was informed of this, an official invitation was sent to the family, who were then seated in the front row at the concert venue. Shahid, as always, was there with his Philips recorder. Halfway through the concert, a drunk official announced, 'Bhairavi! Bhairavi!' Begum Akhtar, in all her modesty, responded with, '*Bhairavi hi toh suna rahi thi, janab* [That's what I was singing, sir].' Hearing this, he exclaimed, '*Bhairavi hai to haye! Haye!*' [Ah, if it's Bhairavi, then splendid!] The phrase 'Bhairavi hai to haye! Haye!' soon turned into an inside joke in the Agha family.[10]

Begum Akhtar always had a Capstan cigarette dangling from her lips. Once, while she was rehearsing, she forgot that there was a lit cigarette pressed between her lips. The cigarette kept burning as she, lost in the melody, played the harmonium. Eventually it burned her lips, but she continued playing. Saleem never smoked in front of his father. Once, when Begum Akhtar was at their house on Eid, she asked him if he smoked. When Saleem said no, and pointed towards his father in the adjacent room, she stood in front of him, covered him and handed him her cigarette.

The poet Kaifi Azmi had said that while watching Begum Akhtar, 'ghazal cannot only be heard, but can also be seen'.[11] She kept her personal life a private matter for most of her life and was an embodiment of her craft. That was what Shahid respected the most about her. Her persona was a spellbinding manifestation of her art. As Regula Burckhardt Qureshi, who knew Begum Akhtar, wrote, 'Not only was she from Lucknow, she epitomized its feudal high culture both in her music and poetry, but also in her speech and manners, as well as in her personal style. Her entire persona evoked a nostalgic, feudal Lucknow.'[12]

Once, Shahid accompanied Begum Akhtar to the studio of All India Radio for a recording session. There, she met a famous singer who was rumoured to be having an affair with his *dhobin* (washerwoman). After she greeted him, in passing, she said: 'Arré,

Khan Sahab, what a clean kurta you're wearing today.' Later, once out of the maestro's sight, they fell over laughing.[13] This incident is a great example of Akhtar's style. Moments like these taught Shahid how he could imbibe the *nakhra* (affectation) and wit of Urdu poetry not only in his poems but also in his persona. It was her influence at that early stage in his career, during the '70s, that brought him closer to the intricacies of Urdu poetry.

Later, Shahid studied the silences, interjections and repetitions in her music, which helped him instil Urdu sensibilities and mannerisms in his poetry. Years later, when he wrote about ghazals in *Ravishing DisUnities: Real Ghazals in English*, an anthology he edited, he also evoked Begum Akhtar's voice and reminisced about how she placed 'the ghazal gently on the raga till it, the raga, opened itself to that whispered love, gave itself willingly, guiding the syllables to the prescribed resting places, till note by syllable, syllable by note, the two merged into yet another compelling ethos. She, in effect, allowed the ghazal to be caressed into music, translated as it were.'[14]

Illustration 8: Shahid and Saleem Kidwai with Begum Akhtar in New Delhi.

Begum Akhtar's presence not only helped shape his poems into a dense contemporary form that resonated with the culture he grew up in, but also offered him an insight into how the political is always hidden in the banal. Once, in a classroom where he was teaching the Urdu ghazal, Shahid narrated the story of how Kaifi Azmi had come to the hotel in New Delhi where Begum Akhtar was staying and recited a line he'd written: 'Once again, the mad lover was sighted in your street.' To which, Begum Akhtar replied, 'Ah! Someone should recite this to Indira Gandhi.'[15] She had instantly recognized the political strength of the line and had equated the 'mad lover' with revolution against power. Although Shahid learnt the art of imbibing the political into the personal from Faiz Ahmad Faiz much later in life, Begum Akhtar had introduced him to the idea.

Shahid had confessed that as a teenager he couldn't bear to be away from Begum Akhtar, that 'in other circumstances you could have said that it was a sexual kind of love—but I don't know what it was. I loved to listen to her, I loved to be with her.'[16] However, this love didn't last long. In 1974, only a few years after Shahid had first met her in Delhi, Begum Akhtar passed away.

She was performing in Ahmedabad on 26 October 1974. Before the concert, she had fever and even though some people suggested she cancel the programme, she was adamant that the show must go on. 'She sang beautifully,' her friend Neelam Gamadia's son Sunil remembers. 'Her voice filled with longing and melancholy as was her trademark. She was wrapping up the performance with her last song and said, "I will now perform my last song, a favourite of my dear friend Neelam." And she sang "Ae Mohabbat Tere Anjaam Pe Rona Aaya", after which she fainted.'[17]

She had suffered a cardiac arrest and was rushed to VS Hospital. Shahid and Saleem were in Delhi when they heard about it. Saleem remembers, 'Abbasi Sahib arrived in the evening to go to Ahmedabad. I picked him up, and we went to

Shanti Hiranand's place, who was one of her students. We were supposed to go the airport, so we were sharing a room. Late at night I heard the phone ring in her study. Early in the morning, when I woke up, Shanti announced that Begum Akhtar had passed away.'

'There was no point in his going to Ahmedabad now,' Saleem says. 'We went to the airport, and Shahid joined us there. The flight to Lucknow was Rs 300–400, I think. We had to borrow money, so that we could go to Lucknow to attend the funeral. At the time, it was a lot of money.'[18]

Once in Lucknow, both Shahid and Saleem stayed up all night at her house. The funeral took place late at night. At one point, Shahid went to one of the bedrooms and started writing an elegy. He later revised it several times, and it was eventually published as 'In Memory of Begum Akhtar', the title poem from the collection. The death scarred him, and he wrote about her in numerous poems, including 'Snow on the Desert' and in the last poem from his final collection, 'I Dream I Am at the Ghat of the Only World'. Begum Akhtar's memory remained in his heart forever, her voice forever echoing in his ears. In his elegy, he wrote:

Your death in every paper,
boxed in the black and white
of photographs, obituaries,

the sky warm, blue, ordinary,
no hint of calamity,

no room for sobs,
even between the lines.

I wish to talk of the end of the world.[19]

Although he only knew her for a brief time, Begum Akhtar's death was the first personal loss that Shahid experienced. 'The true subject of poetry is the loss of the beloved', Faiz had written in a letter to Alun Lewis, circa 1943.[20] Shahid, in his verses, turned into the lover who wrote about the pain of the separation and the loss of the beloved. Whenever he had the chance, Shahid evoked Begum Akhtar in his poems. She remained his muse for the rest of his life, and her voice, which he listened to so often, reminded him of all he had lost.

Decades later, in Tucson, Arizona, as he drove past the fog-covered desert that divided the city very neatly, he realized that he was passing through a unique moment. He tried to find a comparable moment, but there was none. He realized that it was a moment 'which refers only to itself', an incomparable moment. One such unique moment occurred at a Begum Akhtar concert in New Delhi around the time of the Bangladesh Liberation War in 1971, when there was a power cut at the venue. 'The lights went out and there was absolute silence,' Shahid wrote remembering the concert. 'The microphone was also dead. It was an outdoor concert and for a minute or two, the voice was coming from very far away, an echo. And in that echo I heard, with such clarity, something amazing that she used to do with her voice. Just haunting.'[21]

For Shahid, the 'two moments juxtaposed to show that neither can be compared to the other or anything else'. In 'Snow on the Desert', he wrote:

> in New Delhi one night
> as Begum Akhtar sang, the lights went out.

> It was perhaps during the Bangladesh War,
> perhaps there were sirens,

air-raid warnings.
But the audience, hushed, did not stir.

The microphone was dead, but she went on
singing, and her voice

                    was coming from far
away, as if she had already died.

And just before the lights did flood her
again, melting the frost

                    of her diamond
into rays, it was, like this turning dark

of fog, a moment when only a lost sea
can be heard, a time

                    to recollect
every shadow, everything the earth was losing,

a time to think of everything the earth
and I had lost, of all

                    that I would lose,
of all that I was losing.[22]

For the rest of his life, he associated Delhi with Begum Akhtar,
and each time he returned to the city, in his poetry, her voice was
always there. Although he loved the city and its commotion, there
was only so much it could offer. Soon after Akhtari's death in 1974,
Shahid decided to leave for America. He had spent his formative

years in Delhi, had published his first collection in the city, but new experiences and opportunities awaited him elsewhere.

Though a few English-language publications had started emerging in 1970s Delhi, the city offered barely any space for an English poet. There were some English literary circles, but there was limited exposure for a young, emerging poet. Shahid knew from experience that America would offer him much more. In an article titled 'On Teaching English', published in the *Illustrated Weekly of India* in May 1976, Shahid wrote about his time as a professor in Delhi. The article is largely about his teaching philosophy and the educational climate in Delhi, but Shahid's detachment from and weariness with the city is clear in his tone when he writes, 'Here there is no breathing space, total sterility.' Or: 'When my students look at me, so dazed with Yeats, Eliot, Sylvia Plath, I feel like a butcher. I take Sisyphus's rock and roll it in my hands, small enough to stuff down their throats.'[23]

A profile of Shahid published in a magazine called *First City* in February 1991 stated, 'The most marked memories from his days at Delhi University are his attempts at having to justify the studying and teaching of English Literature'; and that for him, 'going to the U.S.A. was the logical answer, particularly because the initial goal seemed well defined: to write his doctorate'.[24] Although he fondly remembered his time in the city and gave credit where it was due—he said in the *First City* profile: 'My years in Delhi were quite happy and I, in many ways, came into my own as a poet for the first time in Delhi'—it was only pragmatic that Shahid would look west for his future endeavours.[25] There was a voice calling for him 'from another country, / where the sea is the most expansive blue', and Shahid had always been aware of that voice.[26]

SEVEN

A Year of Brilliant Water

The time Shahid had spent at Burris Lab in the '60s had a profound impact on him, as it did on Iqbal, who enrolled for a Master of Science in Statistics degree at Ball State University in 1974. Thus, in December 1975, a little more than a year after Begum Akhtar's death, Shahid arrived in America for his PhD at Pennsylvania State University.

Shahid's timing was indeed near perfect: the discourse around a more cosmopolitan and diverse literature in America, one that reflected its 'melting pot of culture', had started to stir, along with a rise in diasporic literature all around the world that focused on immigrants. In hindsight, Shahid had realized that moving to America was a pivotal decision which had placed him in an enviable position where he was simultaneously contributing 'to the new anglophone literatures of the world, the new subcontinental literatures in English and the new multiethnic literatures of the United States'.[1]

Eventually, Shahid ended up contributing to the vocabulary of English poetry in America in ways that perhaps even he hadn't imagined. The move to Penn State had offered Shahid all that the Indian subcontinent couldn't. He had once confessed that at Penn State, he 'grew as a poet, a lover, and a reader',[2] that it was the happiest time of his life. He adapted quickly to life in America.

At Penn State, he lived in an apartment at Atherton Hall, which housed the graduate students, before moving to a studio which had a kitchen. Whenever it was possible, he would cook his favourite delicacies like rogan josh.

The '70s were a time when the first wave of Indian immigrants, mostly doctors, had started moving to America. Although the number of doctors and engineers in this part of the world was high, it wasn't quite the same in the arts. There were very few people from the subcontinent who went overseas for education in those days. Shahid was one of the few South Asians, and the American ecosystem was drastically different from what he was used to in the Indian subcontinent. Naturally, there were cultural differences that Shahid couldn't identify with. He'd said that whatever he saw in America was in a 'satirical way', which provoked him to write light verse.

He took language very seriously and was so attuned to the aesthetics of language that he had an emotional response to each word uttered in his presence. As a poet, he was attentive to each question or comment, which he could turn around with his wordplay. In the '80s, when a woman on the phone asked him why he'd bought the car Nissan Stanza, he had replied: 'Because I'm a poet.' One of the more famous anecdotes from his life is about Shahid having his Wildean moment. The woman at security at Barcelona Airport asked him what he did. He replied: 'I'm a poet.' She then went on to ask what he was doing in Barcelona. To this he responded: 'Writing poetry.' Exhausted by his responses, she asked him if he was carrying anything that could be dangerous to other people on board. Almost as if he had been waiting for the question, Shahid placed a hand on his chest and said: 'Only my heart.' She smiled and let him go.[3]

Sejal Shah, a student from Hamilton College where Shahid later taught, remembers, 'His answering-machine message was simply, "I *knew* you'd call", with emphasis on the "knew". There was no preamble. The first time I heard his message, I hung up. Shahid had, as usual, caught me off guard. The message sounded like a line from one of his poems, like a moment of delight, of enchantment. Hearing his voice left me smiling and speechless.'[4]

While at times it was simply humour that drove him, on other occasions it was also a sort of irreverence. Once, at a used bookstore in Syracuse, Shahid discovered a signed copy of *A Walk Through the Yellow Pages* that he had presented to a married couple. He bought the chapbook and sent it back to them with instructions never to sell it again.

Naturally, humour found its way into his poetry. Although these poems didn't necessarily fit in with the larger body of his work, they shed light on a very different facet of his personality— his sense of humour and wit. Most of his poems deal with loss and nostalgia, but the poems he wrote during his first few years in America—which he called 'The Penn State poems'—focused entirely on all things he found funny. During the first few months of his arrival in the country, he saw advertisements for Bell Telephone (which later became AT&T) that read: 'Has anyone heard from you lately?' and 'It's getting late. Do your friends know where you are?' At one point, Shahid said to himself: 'I have to answer them.' And so he wrote 'The Bell Telephone Hours', a series of five poems, each based on the advertisements. In 'Today, Talk is Cheap. Call Somebody', he wrote:

I said, 'Tell me, Tell me
When is Doomsday?'

He answered, 'God is busy.
He never answers the living.
He has no answers for the dead.
Don't ever call again collect.'[5]

Apart from the fact that these poems are humorous, what made them truly memorable was the way Shahid recited them. He was a natural performer. 'I love to be on display,' as he once said.[6] He wasn't afraid of putting himself out on the stage and could hold everyone's attention for hours. Christopher Merrill wrote about Shahid's recitations: 'He would stop mid-poem to pose for a photograph, exclaiming "I love to be photographed," or to castigate someone in the audience for daring to leave early. More than one embarrassed person returned to their seat after Shahid said, "Are you leaving me? Don't leave me!"'

In one of his recitations, after he had already started reading the third line of a poem, Shahid spotted a classmate sitting in the audience and stopped reading altogether to say 'Hi', after which he went back to reading the poem. Merrill called his dark and irreverent jokes 'stand-up tragedy', for they possessed the knack for causing discomfort in people. But Shahid couldn't care less.[7] There were also times when he introduced his politics into his jokes. He was once reading at Ball State University. It was a small auditorium, and the seats were full. When Shahid entered to read, he saw students sitting on the floor right next to the stage. The first line he uttered was: 'I've always loved the idea of white people at my feet.'[8]

Most of Shahid's friends during the first two years at Penn State were Americans, with the exception of some international students. His closest friends, however, were from the subcontinent. One of them was Anuradha Dingwaney. In 1977, on the day Dingwaney joined Penn State, there was a Shakespeare performance where Shahid was present. After the play, she met Shahid and told him that she recognized him from Delhi and that he had read his poetry at Miranda House in the early '70s, where she was a student. As soon as Shahid heard this, he laughed and said proudly: 'See! She knows me. I don't know her, but she knows me, which means I'm famous.'[9] When Padmini Mongia joined Penn State in the early '80s, she asked the dean of her department about other people from India. She was given two names and phone numbers. The first person she called didn't pick up. The second person was Shahid. They talked on the phone, and since she was at Atherton Hall as well, Shahid invited her over.

'As soon as I saw Shahid for the first time, I knew he was gay,' she recalls. Almost everyone who knew Shahid—all his friends—was aware of this. Padmini remembers that 'there were no two ways and he was very clear about it'.[10] Whenever he spoke of his sexuality, he always did so comfortably and was never affected by anyone else's embarrassment or awkwardness around him.

He had once stated that he realized the fullness of his being in America: 'I had my first full sense of myself as an adult in America. I realized myself as poet, I realized myself as a lover. Many things became fully conscious for me here.'[11] Clearly, Shahid wasn't a person who would hide his sexual orientation. It was a part of him, one that he treated with nonchalance and simply took for granted, no questions asked. Once, when an interviewer asked him what his environment was, Shahid had joked, 'Screw and Let Screw.'[12]

While Shahid had no qualms about his sexual orientation, and there was no anxiety surrounding it, he never wrote about it, for he didn't think it was in line with his poetic pursuits. In an interview, he said: 'It doesn't interest me as a poet, except when it inadvertently appears in my poetry, the way God may appear, or love may appear, or childhood may appear, or anything.'[13] Although this choice might seem anomalous to some, for Shahid, it was quite simple. His experiences of love, loss and anguish are present in his poems, but he was only interested in his life to the extent where it helped him to highlight his poetic concerns and themes.

For Shahid, there was a clear separation between his life and his poetic persona, although they weren't parallel lines and intersected at several points. He was concerned not with his experiences as such but with emotions and ideas that stemmed out of an experience or an event. This is where Eliot's presence is palpable in him, especially Eliot's belief that poetry should be impersonal and distinct from the poet: 'Impressions and experiences which are important for the man may take no place in the poetry [of a mature poet], and those which become important in the poetry may play quite a negligible part in the man, the personality.'[14]

Shahid was of the belief that the value of art was in the work itself, not in the ethnicity, colour, sexual orientation or race of the poet. When he was asked what he thought of 'being defined as a writer of color or other categorization', Shahid responded saying: 'I think it can be a convenient tool at times, but it's finally very boring as a writer. It's interesting that others talk about it, but when you are writing I think you should only be committed to how good you can make your poem, how hard you can work at it, how you can keep developing yourself, transforming yourself, transcending yourself in your work and through your work. I think that's important.'[15] It was a rational and hard-headed decision that Shahid had made, and one that he stood by all his life.

Shahid often said that if one was from a difficult place and if that was the only thing they chose to write about, then they weren't a writer and should stop writing. He didn't believe that propaganda could be used in poetry. In an interview, he once said: 'What I like the most is when somebody is interested in my work not because I am advancing a certain political point of view but because they really can respond to the poetry, to the fullness of the poetry, or respond to the poetry in a full way.'[16] He cited the example of Elizabeth Bishop, a feminist, refusing to be a part of any women's anthologies and said that he sympathized with her strongly. Bishop, whose poems Shahid admired, considered her poetry universal and didn't want to be treated just as a 'woman poet'. She believed that her work was on a par with those of her male contemporaries and that it should be appreciated for its value, not because of her gender. She once wrote in a letter that 'undoubtedly gender does play an important role in the making of any art, but art is art, and to separate writings, paintings, musical compositions, etc., into two sexes is to emphasize values in them that are not art'.[17] This resonates with Shahid's view as well.

Perhaps the only instance where Shahid's sexuality appears in his poems is in the choice of his pronouns. In an interview from the '80s, he said that the 'you' or 'your' in his poetry—'My finger, your phone number / at its tip, dials the night'—was usually an 'amalgamation of lovers', that it wasn't 'strictly autobiographical but it comes from a lot of autobiographical experiences that are collapsed in the poem'.[18] He cited the example of W.H. Auden, who used 'you' in his poetry because he couldn't use 'she'. Shahid did the same in his poems, leaving them ungendered. Although there are some poems on subjects such as mortality where Shahid makes a conscious decision and uses 'him' or 'he', all those poems are set around a theme, in a context or around a question that Shahid wanted people to see in his work.

He was honest and simply didn't want a reductive reading or interpretation of his poems where his poetic concerns and pursuits were discarded and ignored to highlight his sexual orientation. This departure from the path that most modern poets take—where everything was dissolved as one, and the poet's identity becomes the foundation on which the work is built—set Shahid apart not only from his contemporaries but also from those who came before him. As a poet, he wanted his work to be recognized for its inherent quality, not because he was from 'a particular background or ethnicity or sexual orientation'. That, he believed, was 'a disservice to poetry'.[19]

EIGHT

In Exodus, I Love You More

While Shahid was writing his thesis on T.S. Eliot at Penn State, he was also writing poems relentlessly, for he had a lot of time to spare. Although it wasn't the first time Shahid found himself thousands of miles away from the subcontinent, it was the first time he was there of his own accord. Shahid had left for America in December 1975 and didn't return to Kashmir until 1980. During this four-year period, he spoke of Kashmir with the same nostalgia with which Sufia had described her childhood in the plains to Shahid. At Penn State, Shahid came to understand what his mother must have felt when she moved to Kashmir. Sufia often sang songs that she had known from childhood, and Shahid ended up doing something similar in his poems.

History was already prominent in Shahid's poetry, but at Penn State he realized what the conflation of history with memory could do. These poems eventually ended up in his watershed collection *The Half-Inch Himalayas,* which established his position as a promising poet in both the places he called home, the US and the subcontinent, and garnered the attention of eminent writers and poets. One morning in the fall of 1989, the American poet Tess Gallagher phoned Shahid and said, 'Guess who called me last night?' She told him it was Salman Rushdie. Gallagher had mentioned to Rushdie that she was 'reading a book of poems by another subcontinental expatriate, *The Half-Inch Himalayas*.' As soon as Rushdie heard the book's title, she said that he started quoting Shahid's poem 'The Dacca Gauzes' from memory.[1] A year before the phone call, in 1988, Rushdie had written a letter to Shahid, praising his collection:

> Dear Agha Shahid Ali,
>
> Thanks for writing, and I do apologize for not having responded earlier to your book, *The Half-Inch Himalayas*, the more so because I was genuinely struck and impressed by the poems, and even read bits of them aloud to friends. 'The Dacca Gauzes' is, I think, the one that stays most with me: a beautiful piece of work, and the final image unforgettable. Many congratulations—and I hope that, if you are ever in London, you will get in touch.
>
> All the best,
> Salman Rushdie[2]

'The Dacca Gauzes' is one of Shahid's best free-verse poems and marks an important shift in his career. In the poem, while on the one hand he remembers his maternal grandmother's love for muslin, on the other hand he sheds light on the dark colonial past that is attached to the muslin trade. During the seventeenth and eighteenth centuries, Dhaka was the capital of the worldwide muslin trade. However, with the advent of the British rule in India, which coincided with the Industrial Revolution and favoured export of raw cotton and import of manufactured product from Britain, the muslin production in Dhaka had to be stopped. The looms were destroyed.

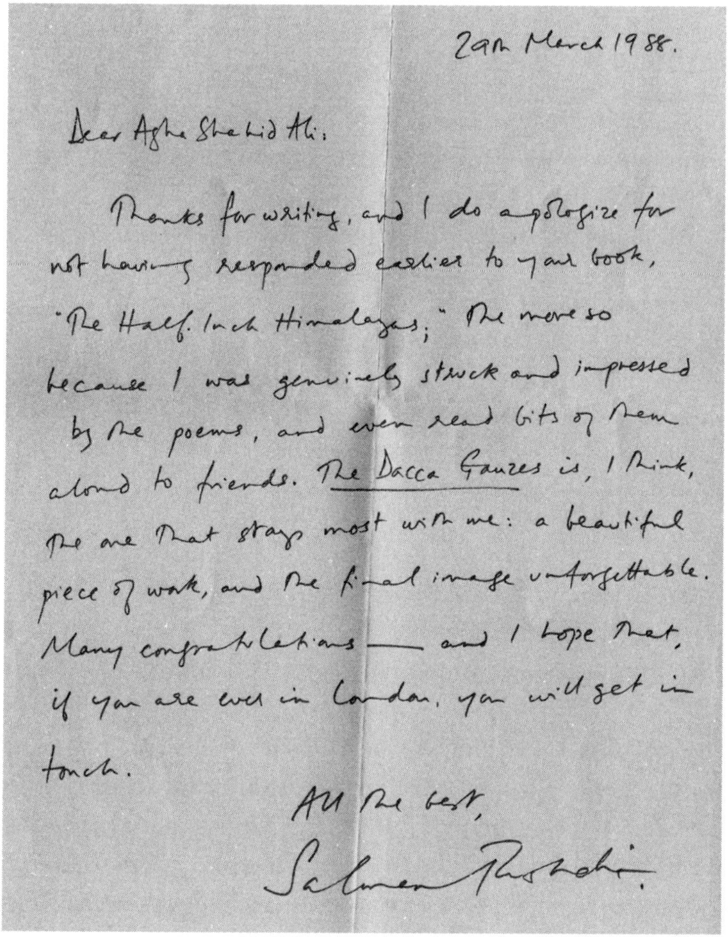

2nd March 1988.

Dear Agha Shahid Ali,

Thanks for writing, and I do apologize for not having responded earlier to your book, "The Half-Inch Himalayas," the more so because I was genuinely struck and impressed by the poems, and even read bits of them aloud to friends. The Dacca Gauzes is, I think, the one that stays most with me: a beautiful piece of work, and the final image unforgettable. Many congratulations — and I hope that, if you are ever in London, you will get in touch.

All the best,

Salman Rushdie

Illustration 9: Salman Rushdie's letter to Shahid, 29 March 1988.

A merchant by the name of William Bolts wrote in 1772 that there had been instances where the thumbs of the weavers had been cut off to stop production.[3] Shahid's poem speaks about a forgotten history and mixes a historical event of the Indian subcontinent with experiences from his childhood:

In history we learned: the hands
of weavers were amputated,
the looms of Bengal silenced,

and the cotton shipped raw
by the British to England.
History of little use to her,

my grandmother just says
how the muslins of today
seem so coarse and that only

in autumn, should one wake up
at dawn to pray, can one
feel that same texture again.

One morning, she says, the air
was dew-starched: she pulled
it absently through her ring.[4]

The reason a figure like Salman Rushdie was deeply impressed by this poem was because, like Rushdie's prose, the poem expresses subcontinental sensibility, rituals and history in the English language. This is seen throughout *The Half-Inch Himalayas*, in Shahid's use of phrases such 'dew-starched' and 'scarlet-women', as well as in his description of the muslins as 'woven air, running / water, evening dew'. For Shahid, who had grown up with English as the primary language in the subcontinent in those days, it was natural that he expressed all his experiences in English with flavours of subcontinental traditions and rituals. He wrote about these rituals and traditions so typical to the subcontinent with great ease—and that's what makes the poems stand out even today.

Poems such as 'A Butcher' and 'At Jama Masjid' are testament to the fact that English is indeed a language of the subcontinent;

they demonstrate the elasticity of the language and how metaphors and idioms from a certain place can be imbibed in it. The Jewish poet Paul Celan had translated a dozen poets before writing his own poetry, breaking the syntax of German in order to express his experience of the Holocaust. This had led the Canadian poet Anne Carson to remark that 'Celan is a poet who uses language as if he is always translating'. Like Celan, Shahid too broke the syntax of English to express his subcontinental experience in a language that he considered his own.

At Penn State, where he stayed for a period of eight years, Shahid devoted a lot of time to writing poetry. In 1981, along with his PhD, he also enrolled for a second master's degree in English at Penn State with an emphasis on writing. By the time he arrived at Penn State, Shahid had started calling himself a poet. *Bone Sculpture* was published in 1972 while *In Memory of Begum Akhtar* was in the pipeline. That was also the period when he grew most as a poet. At Penn State, Shahid learnt that artistic success at a high level required perseverance. He realized the importance of time in poetry. Time was the only way that a poem gained its identity, its own voice. What it led to was a revelation, one that transformed his poetic sensibilities and made him understand that art, after all is said and done, is a process.

Shahid learnt that every poem had a life cycle: from the initial reaction to a phenomenon to the manifestation of emotion in a manner in which it had a certain effect. The best example was his poem 'A Call'. He had been trying to place the poem in a journal for six years before *Cimarron Review*, a magazine that had rejected him on three previous occasions, accepted it. He had painstakingly worked on it after each rejection, and over the years, realized that with each draft the poem became clearer, the questions that he posed became much more complex than before. Shahid had handed several drafts of his poem 'The Dacca Gauzes' to Padmini Mongia and had said to her: 'Keep them safe with you. One day, when I become a famous poet, these will be invaluable.'[5]

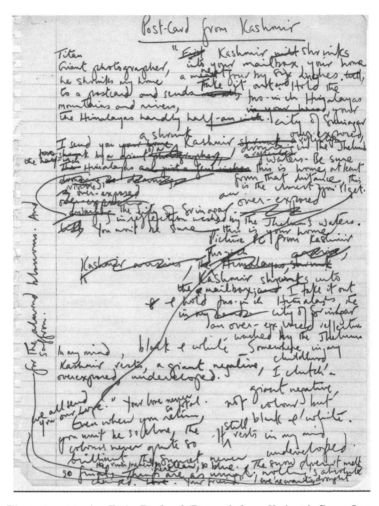

Illustration 10: An Early Draft of 'Postcard from Kashmir', Penn State, October 1979.

While most poets at this stage send their poems to reputed journals and publications, Shahid had something completely different in mind. His goal was to get published in journals whose titles began with each letter of the alphabet: 'When he would get published in, say, *AGNI*, he would say, "Oh, now A is done!" And we'd go to this bar called Corner Room and celebrate,' Anuradha Dingwaney remembers.[6] By the time he died, Shahid had covered all the letters, from A to Z. 'He tried to convince the editor of *Zyzzyva* [a journal that focused on writers and poets from the West Coast of the USA] that he came from a Pacific Rim nation and thus belonged in his pages,' Christopher Merrill recalled in his book *Self-Portrait with Dogwood*. 'His only reservation about becoming a contributing editor to a new literary journal named *Tin House* was its name—he already had his T. Couldn't they consider a name that began with a Z?'[7]

In the '70s, video games had become popular, and Shahid was addicted to *Pac-Man*. Most days, when he wasn't writing, he played *Pac-Man* with Dingwaney and Padmini Mongia at an all-you-can-eat salad bar. But before they'd leave for the restaurant, Shahid would send his poems out for publication. These were the years when he was relentlessly publishing poems in journals and magazines.

'Shahid's process of submitting to journals was remarkable,' Padmini recalls. When he was done with a poem, he decided on four to five journals that he thought would be best for it. However, in those days, one couldn't submit poems simultaneously to all journals, and so Shahid had to wait for an acceptance or a rejection. In the meantime, he continued to revise his poems, and by the time he received a rejection letter, he already had the cover letter ready and knew which journal the poem was going to next. 'There was no room for being crushed by the rejection or taking a couple of days to recover,' Dingwaney remembers. 'He was completely relentless.'

The poems improved in style and language with each version. Shahid had a ritual of checking for letters—especially rejection letters—while leaving or returning to his room. In an interview, he confessed that he never worried about rejections. 'There were zillions of them coming . . . I never took it personally, or maybe I was just shameless,' he said.[8]

Hena Ahmad, Shahid's elder sister, remembers that when Shahid was eighteen, he received a personalized rejection letter from a magazine called *Quest*; the letter said that his poetry was 'far below their standard' and requested that he read more before sending anything again. Through Eliot's influence, Shahid had already learnt that his poetry couldn't be an overflow of emotion and had come to the conclusion that he had to depend more on the trickery of language than on just raw, organic passion. Poetry was an exploration of pure form. Much later, in an essay, he acknowledged as much and wrote: 'Content is achieved sincerity. Sincerity achieved through artifice. Emotion tested by artifice.'[9]

This sincerity and emotion, in Shahid's case, stemmed from memory. Although he was completely at home in America, his memories of Delhi and of his childhood in Kashmir were with him. As soon as Shahid moved to America, he discovered new poets like W.S. Merwin, Charles Simic, Robert Lowell, Adrienne Rich, John Ashbery and James Merrill; their use of language, their formal schemes and how they approached their subjects, deeply influenced Shahid. However, rather than camouflaging with the environment and American mannerisms, Shahid chose to stand out, which made all the difference.

Even though Shahid read American poetry extensively, he didn't allow America's minimalism to water him down and introduced the expansiveness of Urdu poetry into the bloodstream of his writings. His attachment to his roots and the distance from his homeland impacted him deeply. In an essay, Shahid wrote that 'the moon would shine into my dorm room, and I remember one night closing my eyes and feeling I was in my room in Kashmir', and that 'sometimes in a bar at 2:00 a.m., like so many Americans, I felt alone, almost an exile (except when I got lucky!)'.[10] Even though he viewed Penn State as 'a home' if not 'home', looking back at his initial years there, he called his move to America an 'inescapable exile'.[11]

Shahid was never banished from a nation state or exiled because of his political stance; he was simply an immigrant and was aware of that. He also acknowledged that the word exile didn't have the same resonance in the modern-day world; one could simply take a flight and reach home. He was aware that his condition wasn't that of an exile but simply a matter of choice.

As he said in an interview: 'You constantly meet people who are immigrants and who say, oh, I feel like I've lost my culture and I've lost my roots, and I say please don't be so fussy about it. The airplanes work. I mean, if you have a certain kind of income, whether you live in Bombay and fly to Kashmir, or you live in New York and fly to Kashmir, for a certain group it really makes no difference.'[12]

He acknowledged that all this talk about exile was, to some extent, poet-speak, but he also believed that there were psychological consequences of distance that existed beyond the definition of the word émigré. Looking back at his time at Penn State, Shahid said that what he meant by the word exile was 'an entirely new kind of geography, an entirely new kind of sensibility that became available to my poetry . . . [Long pause.] I used 'exile' also because, in some ways, when you write in English, in India, you are in some ways an exile in your own land. In some ways. And I know I'm romanticizing.'[13]

He said that he used the term exile and not expatriate because 'the former is a term with a lot of resonance, because it describes some of the emotional states that the latter would not'.[14] The exilic element is evident in *The Half-Inch Himalayas*. What emerges from the poems is a sense of distance, evident in the title of the collection. The first poem, 'Postcard from Kashmir', which is considered by many as the epigraph to the collection, evokes the 'ultramarine waters' of the Jhelum and provides a sense of perspective from which the poet is looking at the Himalayan mountains that surround Kashmir:

Kashmir shrinks into my mailbox,
my home a neat four by six inches.

I always loved neatness. Now I hold
the half-inch Himalayas in my hand.[15]

Neatly divided into four sections, *The Half-Inch Himalayas* is, structurally, one of his best collections. It truly encompasses the different cultures and landscapes he held in mind during those years and presents a wonderful mix of primarily three places— Kashmir, Delhi and Penn State. Speaking about the poems in the collection some years after its publication, Shahid said that *The Half-Inch Himalayas* was 'a really good book'. It was, he added, 'a really solid book. [There is] nothing [in the book that] I will be embarrassed about.'[16]

The first section of the collection deals entirely with Kashmir, his parents and his ancestors, the second deals with his journey from Kashmir to New Delhi, the history of the Indian subcontinent and its languages. The third focuses on America and the 'movement and loss' he experienced there. And the final section—according to Shahid—is pure nostalgia. The poems about Kashmir from the first section are starkly different from those that appear in the final section. In the first section, Shahid presents memories of his childhood in Kashmir and all that he believed was a vital part of his upbringing.

He started writing about all this and about his time in Delhi at Penn State, thousands of miles away from home. Although he had written some of the poems in Delhi—such as 'After Seeing Kozintsev's *King Lear* in New Delhi' and 'A Butcher'— he perfected them at Penn State. Most of his poems written at Penn State were a manifestation of his past experiences, and it was there, for the first time, that he truly began working with memory.

Yet the four sections are deeply reflective of Shahid's time at Penn State and elucidate how he came to accept America as a home. In poems from the fourth section, like 'The Call', Shahid emerges as a poet who is writing from a faraway land but also as someone who has accepted America as his home. This transition marked an important moment in his career, for from here onwards, Shahid began looking at Kashmir and the subcontinent very differently. This was one of the reasons Shahid was successful in bringing subcontinental flavours to English poetry. In time, he would introduce other elements from the subcontinent to his poetry in different ways, and one of them was through translation. At Penn State, Shahid could feel the absence of Faiz Ahmad Faiz, who was an important part of his upbringing and whose name no one had heard in America.

NINE

A Memory of Musk

When Shahid moved to Penn State, he discovered various American poets and rediscovered poets like Yiannis Ritsos, C.P. Cavafy, Octavio Paz and Osip Mandelstam, whose works he was already aware of. Although there was poetry from all over the world in the United States, it irked Shahid that the American audience was completely oblivious of poets like Faiz and Mahmoud Darwish, whose poems Shahid translated in the '90s at scholar and critic Edward Said's request.

In *Grand Street*, an American magazine, Shahid questioned American poets for their lack of curiosity about poetry from the rest of the world and responded to a *New York Times* article— 'PALESTINIAN'S POEM UNNERVES ISRAELIS'—about Darwish's 'Those Who Pass Between Fleeting Words':

> How many poetry editors, after reading the [*New York*] *Times* story, have solicited translations of the poet? Such a syntax, by keeping the focus on the Israelis, doesn't allow one to ask: So the Palestinians, those terrorists, have poets? And find time, in the midst of oppression, to write poetry? And the PLO has a department of cultural affairs? The *New York Times* is not interested in the culture of the Palestinians nor, really, in that of any of the Arabic-speaking peoples. Nor is much of the

United States. Professors and students in the country's Master of Fine Arts writing programs have read the Israeli poet Yehuda Amichai, but who has heard of Darwish or any other Arab poet? (Some mystically inclined ones know of the nonthreatening Kahlil Gibran.)[1]

Though he took on the task of translating Darwish's poems in the '90s, Shahid's primary concern in the '80s was Faiz. According to the poet Naomi Shihab Nye, Faiz's name was 'mentioned in Pakistan as much as the sun'.[2] He was a poet of world stature, comparable to the likes of Pablo Neruda, Nazim Hikmet, César Vallejo and Yannis Ritsos. He was arguably the greatest Urdu poet of his time, one who wrote about the oppressed, no matter which community, country or religion they belonged to, and was as respected in India as he was in Pakistan. He was widely appreciated in Kashmir, where he finished his poem 'Subh-e-Azadi'.

Faiz was a poet no one could ignore. In 1958, when the Pakistani president Ayub Khan—who had sent Faiz to jail—was asked by UNESCO for a writer or poet from Pakistan for a series of translations into major world languages, Khan had nominated Faiz. Even though Khan didn't agree with Faiz's politics, he respected his poetry and his international reputation. Shortly after the translations, Faiz was awarded the Lenin Peace Prize. After the death of Zulfikar Bhutto, Faiz left for Beirut, where he spent time with Edward Said and a fellow Pakistani, the political thinker Eqbal Ahmad. In *Reflections on Exile and Other Essays*, Said mentioned Faiz and wrote about his stature as a world poet:

> The crucial thing to understand about Faiz . . . is that like Garcia Marquez he was read and listened to both by the literary elite and by the masses. His major—indeed it is unique in any language—achievement was to have created a contrapuntal rhetoric and rhythm whereby he would use classical forms

(qasida, ghazal, masnavi, qita) and transform them before his readers rather than break from the old forms. You could hear old and new together. His purity and precision were astonishing, and you must imagine therefore a poet whose poetry combined the sensuousness of Yeats with the power of Neruda. He was, I think, one of the greatest poets of this century, and was honoured as such throughout the major part of Asia and Africa.[3]

'To have to introduce Faiz's name seemed a terrible insult to a very significant element of my culture,' Shahid once wrote.[4] For him, Faiz was a poet who stood out for numerous reasons. During Shahid's formative years, Faiz's poems were recited on both sides of the India–Pakistan border, by all classes of people from all walks of life. Faiz's words were summoned at every occasion, for they resonated with the sentiments of millions of people.

But there were other reasons, more personal, that made Faiz even more important to Shahid. Faiz had stayed at Shahid's house in Srinagar before Partition and sent a copy of *Zindan-Nama* to Ashraf when it was published. Faiz's poems had inflicted on the young Shahid what Harold Bloom called the 'immortal wound'— one that pierces the heart and from which one cannot recover.

While Shahid had already internalized Faiz's verses in his father's voice as a young boy, Begum Akhtar had accentuated his love for Faiz. 'Begum Akhtar comes back to me in strange moments. As does Faiz. Often, the two come back together,' Shahid once said.[5] For someone who felt this way about Faiz, it was indeed appalling to note the poet's absence from the West's cultural landscape.

Thus, in September 1980, Shahid wrote a letter to Faiz, asking him for permission to translate his poems. Faiz had, at the time, been exiled by General Zia-ul-Haq and had found a home in Beirut, where he was an editor with the *Lotus Magazine*, a trilingual journal of international literature jointly funded by the Soviet Union, Egypt, East Germany and the Palestine Liberation

Organization. In the letter asking if he could translate the poems, Shahid reminded Faiz that he had lived at their house in Srinagar and bribed him with a rare tape of Begum Akhtar singing his ghazals. In two weeks, Faiz replied: 'You are welcome to make your adaptations of my poems which I shall be happy to receive.'[6]

Chief - Editor

LOTUS

Journal of Afro - Asian
Writers Association
(English - French - Arabic)

P.O.B. 135/430
BEIRUT - LEBANON
Tel : 800011 - 800211

Date October 6, 1980

Ref.

Mr. Agha Shahid Ali
275 Atherton Hall
The Pennsylvania State University
University Park, Pennsylvania 16802
U.S.A

My Dear Shahid:

Thank you for your letter of 6th September.

I certainly knew your father and I am glad to have news from you.

You are welcome to make your adaptations of my poems which I shall be happy to receive. Also some of your own poems and the tape or cassette of Begum Akhtar which you have kindly offered to send.

With kind regards.

Yours sincerely,

Faiz Ahmed Faiz

FAF/rs

Illustration 11: Faiz Ahmad Faiz's letter to Shahid, 6 October 1980.

As soon as he received the response, Shahid started translating Faiz. Although he had started working on the translations at Penn State after receiving Faiz's letter in 1980, the best of this project would only come out in the late '80s. After 1987, when Shahid came to Kashmir during his summer vacations (he was teaching at Hamilton College at the time), his mother would help him with the translations. The process was quite simple: they selected the poems that would best suit the English language through trial and error, and then came up with the transliterated versions, which Shahid would work on for months. 'There were times when he would spend days and days on one line,' Shahid's sister Hena recalls. 'One time, I woke up at 5 a.m. and saw that the light in his room was on—Bhaiya had stayed up all night working on one line. Just one line. Imagine! That was the level of precision involved.'[7]

From his initial attempts, Shahid had realized that there was no way in which the Urdu, especially Faiz's Urdu, could be replicated in the English language. Reading the translations of various Urdu and Persian poets in English, he had become aware that his task as a translator was not to carry out a literal translation but to domesticate Faiz in English. Shahid knew that he was translating for the American audience and believed that the translation should, for all its links with the Urdu original, read like an English poem, have a flow of its own and its own aesthetic identity. When Shahid came across the translations of Faiz done by Victor Kiernan, he felt that while Kiernan's work was essential and that he had managed to transfer all the meaning residing in the originals, it was not poetry. Shahid felt that Faiz had been made to sound stilted in the English language, that Faiz's voice was constrained by the words Kiernan had used, that the translations were quite literal, and took away the rhythm and the essence present in the Urdu originals.

Not only was Shahid translating Faiz, he was also one of the reasons for Faiz's popularity in America. Soon after Shahid wrote to Faiz in 1980, he came across Naomi Lazard's translations of some of Faiz's poems in a journal called *Kayak*, and eventually started corresponding with her. She had met Faiz at a literary conference in Honolulu, and as soon as she did, Lazard knew she was around a major poet. Whenever they got some free time, they would sit down to translate his poems. Faiz himself explained to her what his poems meant, what they could mean. 'There were cultural differences. What was crystal clear to an Urdu-speaking reader meant nothing at all to an American. I had to know the meaning of every nuance to re-create the poem,' she wrote in the introduction to *The True Subject: Selected Poems of Faiz Ahmad Faiz.*

After the conference, Lazard asked Faiz for his address, so that the translation could continue over letters. Faiz told her that she didn't need it, and that if she addressed her letter to 'Faiz, Pakistan', it would reach him. The correspondence continued, and so did the translation process.[8]

When Lazard—who published her translations of Faiz in 1988 as *The True Subject: Selected Poems of Faiz Ahmad Faiz*—applied for a fellowship for her translations, the National Endowment for the Arts rejected her application stating that the panellists were not convinced of the literary importance of her project.[9] Shahid corresponded with Lazard after he found out about her project and praised her attempts and perseverance. 'Her lack of knowledge of Urdu doesn't seem to have been a handicap,' Shahid wrote in response to her essay 'Translating Faiz', published in *Columbia,*[10] and in his review of the book published in *Grand Street*, he commended her efforts to introduce Faiz to America, writing that Lazard had done 'brave and lonely work'.[11]

Shahid praised her translations, but in the introduction to *The Rebel's Silhouette: Selected Poems*—Shahid's translation of Faiz's poetry—he also suggested that 'someone who doesn't know the language he is translating from can never truly know the extent of his failure or triumph'.[12] While translating Faiz's poems, Shahid had come across W.S. Merwin's translations of Mirza Ghalib, which were commissioned by the Pakistani critic Aijaz Ahmad for an American audience and for the centennial of Ghalib's death.

'What emerged was sometimes spectacular, sometimes magical, sometimes passable—but always interesting. Merwin and Rich's efforts struck me as particularly compelling, some of which have inspired me in my attempts,' Shahid wrote in the introduction to the translation.[13]

This example led Shahid to proclaim that it wasn't crucial for the translator to understand the language from which they were translating, but they needed to be the 'poet of the language' into which they were translating. Yet at the same time, he felt that translating the duality of meaning from Urdu was a task only for someone who could understand the language. Even though he thought Lazard's translations were as close as one could get to Faiz, and that one could sense through them her loyalty towards the originals and her love for the poet, Shahid believed that there was room for improvement. In Lazard's translations, some elements of Faiz's poetry were missing, he felt.

Shahid wanted to capture Faiz's emotional excitement, recreate his energy in English, for which he took some liberties, leaving a line, adding a word and even taking a line from the bottom and placing it on top. Shahid's version of 'Evening' is as close as anyone has got to the Urdu original's rhythm, flow and energy. In the translation, he rearranges the lines—placing 'history to tear itself from this net' before 'silence to break its chains', so that the 'silence' line is followed by 'a symphony of conch shells'— and the thought comes full circle:

> The sky waits for this spell to be broken,
> for history to tear itself from this net,
> for Silence to break its chains
> so that a symphony of conch shells
> may wake up the statues
> and a beautiful, dark goddess,
> her anklets echoing, may unveil herself.

Faiz had, like Ghalib and Muhammad Iqbal, exquisitely broken the diction of Urdu poetry and endowed it with a new flair by transcending traditional use of the Urdu language. Naomi Lazard had written in Faiz's obituary, 'In Pakistan, under the censorship of various dictatorships, including the present one, it is impossible to call things by their right names.'[14] While Faiz was writing within the realms of a tradition, he was also revolutionizing the tradition from within. Urdu poetry had mostly confined itself to themes like love and longing for the beloved (the beloved can be god, friend or lover). But Faiz pushed it into a political realm by bringing in the idea of revolution. However, he never broke away from the tradition of Urdu poetry. In his verses, the beloved is the lover and the friend but also the revolution. He announced this departure through his poem 'Mujh Se Pehli Si Mohabbat', which Shahid translated as 'Don't Ask Me, My Love, for That Love Again'.

In his introduction to *The Rebel's Silhouette*, he pointed out that Faiz makes use of phrases that can mean two things at once.[15] He noted that the words '*tera dard*' can be read as 'the sorrow you've caused' as well as 'the sorrow you feel', which poses a problem for Western translators who aren't comfortable with Urdu. Lazard translated the line '*tera gham hai to gham-e-dahar ka jhagra kya hai*' as 'The torments of the world meant nothing; / you alone could make me suffer'; and Kiernan translated it as 'The time's pain nothing, you alone were pain'—but both of them fail to address the duality of 'your sorrow'. Shahid tackled it by extending it to three lines: 'How could one weep for sorrows other than yours? / How could one have any sorrow but the one you gave? / So what were these protests, these rumours of injustice?'

When Faiz died in 1984, Shahid wrote an elegy for him which was published in *The Half-Inch Himalayas*. In it, he referred to his correspondence with Faiz, how he grew up with Faiz's words flowing through his veins as blood, and how Faiz 'became, like memory, necessary':

Twenty days before your death you finally
wrote, this time from Lahore, that after the sack

of Beirut you had no address . . . I
had gone from poem to poem, and found

you once, terribly alone, speaking
to yourself: 'Bolt your doors, Sad heart! Put out

the candles, break all cups of wine. No one,
now no one will ever return.'[16]

Translating Faiz opened up a new world of possibilities for Shahid.
As he translated, he refined the ways in which to weave Faiz's
sensibility into the fabric of the English language. He understood
the elasticity of English and knew how he could incorporate his
concerns into the poems while still staying true to their origins.

In fables, one hears of Arabic, Urdu and Persian poets who
were asked by their masters to memorize thousands of verses of
other poets only to forget them before writing their own. This
practice allowed them to learn from their precursors and to keep
the tradition alive. Doing so, they expanded the universe of
the metaphors available to them, and at the same time, it gave
them a barometer against which they could measure their works.
Translation was a similar exercise for Shahid. While he translated
and expressed his precursor's subcontinental voice in English,
he realized the manners in which his own experiences could be
expressed in the language. It was similar to Merwin's case—
translating gave him more control over English, so much so that
it led Shahid to declare, in an interview, that 'Merwin became
Merwin-esque by translating'.[17]

In the late '40s, the eighteen-year-old Merwin made a
pilgrimage to Saint Elizabeth Hospital in Washington, DC to

meet another poet, Ezra Pound. Although Pound was under indictment for treason against the United States—following radio broadcasts during the Second World War where he had declared his support for Benito Mussolini—Merwin admired the poet and had wandered into the hospital looking for advice from a revered figure. Pound began by saying that if Merwin was serious about being a poet, he should write seventy-five lines every day. 'At your age you don't have anything to write about,' Pound continued. 'You may think you do, but you don't. So get to translating.'[18]

In a career that spanned almost seven decades, Merwin followed Pound's advice to learn the art of translation. He translated poetry into English, from languages including German, Russian, Chinese, Egyptian, Welsh, Urdu, Japanese, Persian and Sanskrit. Shahid finds himself in this exquisite lineage of poets who broke the barriers of language from within by translating. Shahid had, like Merwin, become Shahid-esque by translating and had returned like the 'wanderer from the mountain slopes' with a new language, as Rainer Marie Rilke wrote in 'The Ninth Elegy':

> For when the traveler returns from the mountain slopes into the valley, he brings, not a handful of earth, unsayable to others, but instead some word he has gained, some pure word, the yellow and blue gentian.

By the time Shahid turned to his own poems, he had gained an understanding of not only Urdu but also English. By extending his subcontinental sensibility that was steeped in Urdu traditions, he helped break the boundaries of English poetry, introducing new ideas and themes that enriched the language. 'Poetry is what is gained in translation,' Joseph Brodsky had stated,[19] and Shahid understood how translation, too, was a way of extending the language. Translation allowed him to recreate moments from his

'Urdu past', in a language that he refined and honed, touching the geographies and languages he belonged to.

Translating the works of Faiz allowed Shahid to discover an idiom that was inflected by his Urdu, Kashmiri and Hindi pasts. In this idiom, he could express his politics as well as his love. Faiz, who had reinvented Urdu for contemporary times and let his language absorb his politics, had done the same within the realm of a tradition that could be traced back to the great Urdu poets such as Muhammad Iqbal, Mirza Ghalib and Mir Taqi Mir. It was tradition that turned Shahid into the poet he was: the tradition he belonged to, the tradition that transformed him and the tradition that, like Faiz, he ended up transforming.

TEN

A Route of Evanescence

In 1983, after spending almost eight years at Penn State, Shahid moved to Tucson, Arizona for an MFA degree in creative writing. The astonishing south-western landscape had a profound effect on him, as they'd had on the painter Georgia O'Keeffe when she arrived in New Mexico for the first time in 1929. O'Keeffe was mesmerized by the landscapes. In a letter to her husband, Alfred Stieglitz, she expressed her love for the place: 'When I got to New Mexico, that was mine. As soon as I saw it that was my country. I'd never seen anything like it before, but it fitted to me exactly. It's something that's in the air—it's different. The sky is different, the wind is different. I shouldn't say too much about it because other people may be interested and I don't want them interested.'[1]

Three years after Stieglitz's death in 1949, O'Keeffe permanently moved to New Mexico, for it was there, away from the cityscape of New York, that she found a landscape to paint. Titles of O'Keeffe's paintings made their way into Shahid's poems. He once joked that he wanted to write a poem about O'Keeffe's 'vaginal petals'.[2] Shahid, who admired O'Keeffe's works and quoted from her letters, responded to Arizona in a similar manner. For him, it was a place where it was 'always yesterday, no daylight savings there', and it felt 'strangely out of time'.[3]

In Tucson, Shahid received an offer from the University of Michigan Press for the publication of his doctoral thesis. Although Shahid hadn't sent it for publication, they had selected his thesis, *L'Entre Deux Guerres: T.S. Eliot as Editor*, on merit. (Shahid spent a lot of time converting the thesis into a book.) By the mid-'80s, he had also started responding to his environment. Tucson was where he witnessed the monsoon again, and it reminded him of the city of his birth, Delhi. 'Rain has had a profound impact on me, as I'm sure it has had on many people,' he said in an interview, '[and] when I went to Arizona there was this flood. I arrived and there was rain for two weeks. It was unusual in the desert and they called it monsoons.'[4]

The rain and the vast landscape reminded Shahid of all that was absent from Penn State. After Kashmir, Arizona was the place that gave Shahid something to write about. American poet Christopher Merrill, whom Shahid met at the Bread Loaf Writers' Conference in Middlebury, Vermont in the early '80s, recalls that though topography and nature were never among Shahid's concerns, the rain and the desert offered him something to write about, and he used them to express something much more humane.[5] In an early version of 'I Dream I Return to Tucson in the Monsoons', Shahid wrote:

> There is nothing but silence
> around me only the dark mountains.
> Then someone lights a match. It dies.
> 'Who are you?' I cry out,
> and the moon touches my shoulder.
> From behind the saguaros,
> he steps into its light,
> the hair on his arms turning to water.
> 'Who were you, tell me, who are you?'

The moon is turning the desert to water,
and the tide is full. I ask,
'Why is there no rain?'[6]

In 1985, Shahid obtained his MFA degree from the University of Arizona. He had decided, by this time, that he wanted to stay on in America. In a letter to his father, written in January 1985, Shahid stated that getting a job as a professor was very tough at the time but returning to India wasn't an option, because as a professor in India he would be 'too busy wondering how to finance even a bottle of Scotch'.[7] Thus, when his roommate Steve Moddelmog's wife, Hala, offered him a position as an English trainer at a company called JNC Communications, Shahid accepted it. In Tucson, he continued writing poems, became the editorial assistant for the *Sonora Review* and continuously engaged with poetry, working on the drafts of the poems from *The Half-Inch Himalayas* and *A Walk Through the Yellow Pages*. It was here that he finally, after a long spell, learnt to drive—something that he thought had turned into 'a marvellous personality plus'[8] for him—and bought a 1983 Sentra. Justifying this decision, he wrote in a letter to his father:

> I want to be in America for a few more years, and make some money. As you know, one cannot really make money in India—not as a professor. Once I have a green card, I could come to India every year for at least three months. That would be almost like my coming for the summer from Delhi—the way I did for seven years. In terms of the world situation, I don't think it makes much difference whether I come from Delhi or from New York. And the thing is this: if I were in India, I would not be able to lead a swanky enough lifestyle. Could I? But given the international economy and the importance of the dollar, I could, whenever I visit India, be lavish. And that is what

I want. So look at it this way: I would come to India for three months every summer and then you both could come here in the winters. Or autumns . . .

As a poet writing in English, I find the scene here, that is, the literary scene, much more alive. There are all these things in my mind. So, as Faiz says, Chand roz aur mere jaan, chand roz!⁹

In Tucson, no matter where he looked, nostalgia was all he found. All the experiences from the south-west—the people he met, those who had died while he was there, and the narratives of those who had lived there for centuries or had died centuries ago—manifested themselves in *A Nostalgist's Map of America*. In the poems written in Tucson, Shahid explores history, myth and injustice with a subliminal nostalgia. His vocabulary is that of loss and suggests all that could have been. In an endorsement, James Merrill, whom Shahid would become friends with in 1987, wrote:

There are Mogul palace ceilings whose countless mirrored convexities at once reduce, multiply, scatter and enchant the figures under their spell. If I may speak for 'America', it is a privilege to be held in so mercurial, many-faceted a gaze as this poet's, who goes to the heart of my troubles and turns them into bitter honey.¹⁰

Shahid had always been fascinated by historical events, and when he came to the south-west, he was curious about its history. There, he found out about the Penitentes—a people belonging to a tribe in the Sangre de Cristo Mountains of New Mexico who are nomadic, Hispanic and Catholics, and are known for their re-enactments of the crucifixion every Easter. For this re-enactment ritual, a boy—always a bachelor—is chosen as Christ, and he carries the cross. If during the process the boy dies, they leave his sandals outside his parents' home, so they know their son has died, and his grave remains a secret for a year. Shahid responded to the ritual with 'Crucifixion', a poem in which he talks about the ritual and the bachelor who is 'lashed with ropes soaked in water, blood running / down his back'.

Another event was the Bisbee Deportation of 1917, which led him to the poem 'The Keeper of the Dead Hotel'. In 1917, the copper-mining town of Bisbee, Arizona turned into a ghost town following a major deportation of mineworkers. 'There was a strike there in 1917, which was put down really brutally and people in Bisbee don't like to talk about it now,' Shahid said at a poetry reading at Ball State University in 1997, '. . . first it was put down, then all the surviving male members of families were put into box cars and sent away to the New Mexican desert 100 miles away. And so their families had to leave Bisbee to look for these men and there are pictures of the trains, it looks like a scene out of Nazi Germany.'[11] The incident moved Shahid, and he ended up writing 'The Keeper of the Dead Hotel', a mix of fantasy and fact, shot with a certain kind of nostalgia for a past that he had never lived in.

He conveys a sense of calm and composure when he takes on the voice of the last speaker of a language (in 'Someone Wants Me to Live'), or, at times, when he traces the landscapes and the terrains of the ghost towns of Arizona and their histories ('The Keeper of the Dead Hotel'). There is always a wonderful ease with which he maintains a distance from the subject, while at the same time capturing a lost past. When he writes about his friend from Penn State, Philip Paul Orlando, who died of AIDS in the late '80s—'Now there's only regret: I didn't send you / My routes of Evanescence. You never wrote'—there is the same composure.[12]

Although Orlando was an undergraduate and Shahid a graduate student, they were good friends. The last time they met was in 1979, when Orlando graduated. Then, in 1985, 'out of the blue', Shahid got a call from him in Tucson. Orlando said that he and his lover were moving to California, that they were driving

from Boston to California and would come to see him, which they
did. Six months later, Shahid received a call from him. He said
he had to tell Shahid something. 'I said "don't". I knew he had
called to tell me he had AIDS. It had quite an effect on me that
someone who had become a part of the ghostly patterns of the
past suddenly came back into my life and died more vividly. And
of course, died of this horrible disease.'[13] In 'A Nostalgist's Map
of America', Shahid wrote about the call. But more importantly,
it was here that Shahid described his relationship with Orlando:

> Please forgive me Phil, but I thought
> of your pain as a formal feeling, one
> useful for the letting go, your transfusions
>
> mere wings to me, the push of numerous
> hummingbirds, souvenirs of Evanescence
> seen disappearing down a rout of veins
> in an electric rush of cochineal.[14]

For the first time in his poetry, Shahid put into words how he
approached a subject matter. It was never a spontaneous rush
of emotions or a feeling that he expressed in his verses, but an
investigation of nostalgia, loss or grief. The comparison of the
transfusions with 'mere wings', as well as the line 'rush of cochineal',
are references to Emily Dickinson's poem 'Routes of Evanescence'.
'I would eat evanescence slowly,' Dickinson had written in a letter to
her sister in 1857, almost five years before she wrote the first draft of
the poem capturing the movement of a hummingbird.[15]

In Arizona's landscapes and conversations, all that Shahid
secured was evanescence. Even though the poems he wrote were
sentimental and emotional, he, as a poet, was never sentimental.
The elegiac power in his poems came from distance, and how he
approached the people and events he wrote about. When Shahid

wrote 'It was a year of brilliant water', or 'We must always have a place / to store the darkness', he knew what words would suggest a feeling and convey the right emotion to the reader. Unlike the works of most modern poets, Shahid's poems were never about incidents from his life—he wrote out of experience, not about it— and thus, he chose moments with care and delicacy, weaving them into lines that he believed were beautiful.

His poetic concerns, on the other hand, were constantly evolving. Shahid said in an interview, 'When I look at *The Half-Inch*, I can't foresee *A Nostalgist's Map* and when at the latter, I can't foresee *Country*. Hindsight can lead one to see the developments as maybe inevitable—that is, to see the continual presence of concerns now diluted, now refined, enhanced.'[16] Clearly, some of Shahid's concerns as a poet kept changing. His work was often influenced by the land he was living in, by the names of places that forced him to respond, that demanded a poem.

In 1987, Shahid received offers for teaching positions from various universities. Ever since he had completed his MFA, he wanted a job at a university in America. Finally, he chose Hamilton College in Clinton, New York, where he was appointed as assistant professor of English. Rather than taking a flight from Tucson, Shahid decided to drive to Clinton and was advised to buy a car. So he purchased a Ford Bronco II.

Two months before he left Tucson, a relationship that he was in fell apart, and Shahid was devastated. At a poetry reading he narrated all that followed: 'Oh, Shahid! Here's your chance to act really macho and get into your Bronco II and drive across America with your sunglasses on. But driving, what really happened was I ended up crying, listening to *The Way We Were*, listening to Barbra Streisand.'[17] He narrated this anecdote at each reading following the publication of *A Nostalgist's Map of America*, not only because it was funny, but because it led him to so many poems that he eventually included in the collection.

While driving across America, he travelled through small towns and cities and was fascinated by their names. His favourite, unsurprisingly, was the city called Truth or Consequences in New Mexico. In a reading, he said, 'I was delighted to know that in Oregon, there is Madras [Mad-russ], which we know as Madras [Mad-raas] in India, and it is one hour away from Damascus, which if you're interested in rhyming, which I am, there is something for you to work on.'[18]

On his drive, he recognized what most Americans would simply miss, and what most subcontinental people would laugh at. In his poem, he captured his hyphenated identity as it manifested in the names of places in another continent. Driving on Route 80 in America, he dreamt of India:

When on Route 80 in Ohio
I came across an exit
to Calcutta

the temptation to write a poem
led me past the exit
so I could say

India always exists
off the turnpikes
of America

so I could say
I did take the exit
and crossed Howrah

and even mention the Ganges
as it continued its sobbing
under the bridge[19]

While a major chunk of poems from the collection were written in Tucson, Shahid worked on them for a long time. In 1991, while he was still at Hamilton, *A Nostalgist's Map of America* was published by Norton and included poems like 'Snow on the Desert'. Placed against his entire body of work, the poem is significant for it marks a departure in his poetry. Reading the poems written before and after 'Snow on the Desert', it becomes evident that this poem, with its end-rhymes and metaphors, was where he started becoming more interested in form. This turn towards formalism was, to some extent, because of the presence of James Merrill, a figure whom Shahid grew closer to during his time at Hamilton.

ELEVEN

Shahid, the Teacher

In 1987, during his job interview at Hamilton, Shahid met Patricia O'Neill for the first time. She remembers that Shahid charmed everyone with his 'sense of humour backed by a thorough knowledge of English and American literary history'.[1] Like Shahid, she too was a junior faculty member in what she called a 'department dominated by old white male colleagues'.[2] Both of them loved Keats and Shelley. Shahid had rented an apartment very close to where she lived, and they would go on long jogs around the campus together. As it would turn out, Shahid soon became one of the most sought-after professors in the department.

The Pakistani novelist Kamila Shamsie was one of Shahid's students at Hamilton. Later, when Shahid moved to the University of Massachusetts (UMass) in 1993, she, along with another student Anthony Lacavaro, followed him there. Although Shahid didn't teach Kamila at UMass, she took a course that Shahid was teaching at Hamilton. As she recalls, 'On the first day of the Introduction to Creative Writing class, he told the sixteen of us in the room that he wanted us to become so attuned to the aesthetics of language that by the end of the semester we would be unable to hear a single word without registering a reaction to it.'[3]

Illustration 12: Shahid with Patricia O'Neill at Hamilton College, Clinton, New York.

Shahid was extremely serious and dedicated to his job. The outlines for his courses were rigorous, and he included everyone from Allen Ginsberg to T.S. Eliot and James Merrill in the syllabus. He detailed each step and made it clear what the students were required to do: it was indeed demanding. Shahid despised the term 'creative writing' and preferred 'imaginative writing' instead, because the word 'creative' struck him 'as not altogether precise'. 'I teach creatiff writing,' he once joked to publisher Rukun Advani.[4]

Although Shahid knew that his opinion was purely subjective, he believed that poets are born and not created, that poets are 'certainly not created in a classroom though those who have it in them may suddenly realize a thing or two in that environment'.[5] But Shahid's teaching philosophy was quite clear, as he mentioned in an essay. 'I want them to disagree with me, to challenge my assumptions. But I want them to be catholic and generous when they do so.'[6]

However, at times, he was also quite ruthless. 'This line should be put against a wall and shot,' he once famously told a student

at a writing workshop, an anecdote that came to be repeated by
almost everyone who knew him.[7] He would carefully critique the
poems written by his students and work on their lines and stanzas
meticulously. He would jot down notes and suggestions pertaining
to each line in the margins, circle words with question marks and
cut out bits that he thought added nothing to the poem. Sejal
Shah, one of his students at Amherst, noted, 'Shahid often rewrote
our poems, starting from the bottom, working his way to the top.
He suggested new possibilities for each of us, and read them in
his lilting voice. This rewriting occasionally hurt my feelings,
bewildered me, and sometimes made me furious.' Looking at
Shah's poem 'Alexander Street', Shahid asked her to make the
last line the first, and in another one, a twenty-five-line poem, he
crossed out so many lines that only eight remained.[8]

Shahid was indeed ruthless when he edited these works, which
often broke the hearts of his students, who had written the poems
with love, care and attention. But soon enough, all of them realized
that what he was doing was necessary and constructive criticism.
And he would, unlike other professors at Hamilton College, call his
students over to his house for dinners, where they would continue to
discuss poetry. Academics, poets, his friends and his students would
all come for dinner at his place, and he would cook for all of them.

'He invited us and other friends over for hours-long, sprawling
dinner parties,' Shah wrote. 'People spilled over from room to
room—Shahid had many friends and admirers, and we all basked
in his glow . . . One night, when the stove burners were not
working and the food had to be warmed up elsewhere, Shahid
charmed us as any good host would, playing Hindi film music and
ABBA. No one minded not eating for a while—we may not have
even noticed. I remember he broke into song . . .'[9]

He was a generous teacher who never played favourites, but
he was also quite masterful in the way he handled things. Shamsie
remembers:

He told us of a student who came to Shahid to contest a grade: 'He said, "I think I should have got an A." And he went on about how his grade should have been higher. So, I said, okay, if you want an A sing "Achy Breaky Heart" to me.' (That song was a recent hit at the time). 'So, he sang the song, and I raised his grade. I wanted him to know that I really couldn't be bothered to stand there arguing about his grade, but he wasn't getting an A for his writing.' That sums up a particular facet of Shahid—it was all very funny, but he had a point to make. And I don't imagine anyone who heard him tell that story would have gone to him asking to have their grade changed.[10]

Illustration 13: Shahid with Kamila Shamsie, Northampton, Massachusetts, 10 December 1997.

American poet Jason Schneiderman, another of Shahid's students, says, 'At his first craft lecture at NYU, Shahid was arguing for the importance of reading canonical texts alongside contemporary literature, and he kept insisting that we would be shocked by his insistence on the value of dead white male writers. I recall being charmed rather than shocked, and we kept saying things like, "But Shahid, we read Milton!" He was trying to articulate a theory of poetry as charged language. This was at the tail end of the '90s (I think it was spring 2000 or fall 2000), and a strong form of identity politics was shifting back to a kind of slightly reconstructed universal humanism. He was doing his best to be provocative, but he was so performative in his provocation, that we were all endeared, rather than provoked.'[11]

In class, he would try and bind his students in questions of form, while at the same time teaching them the likes of Allen Ginsberg, who had completely rebelled against all formal constraints in his poetry. The students were asked to write villanelles and ghazals, and to even turn newspaper articles into poems. 'He did teach Merrill, and I didn't understand Merrill at all,' Schneiderman remembers. 'Shahid would explain his formal experiments to us, and I thought they sounded completely absurd.'[12]

'One day,' Shamsie recalls, 'Shahid brought in a *New York Times* article about a man who worked for Amnesty International, and he said we had to write a poem that only used words that were in the article—we weren't allowed to even change the tense of a verb.'[13] Shahid was trying to bind them in the shackles of form so that they could be eventually liberated. He brought them closer to formal poetry, with which he had started experimenting. To express oneself elegantly in a formal poem was—and still is—a challenge that many poets took on. Shahid did the same in the late '80s, after he came in contact with James Merrill.

TWELVE

My Dearest James

Sometime in the '90s, Shahid wrote a poem about the Bosnian War and sent it to James Merrill, who responded saying, 'There is nothing that you can do about Bosnia, but the least you can do is write a good poem.'[1] Merrill's influence on Shahid during the late '80s and early '90s again changed the manner in which Shahid approached poetry. This was one of the strongest friendships in Shahid's life.

Although they became friends when Shahid started teaching at Hamilton College, Shahid met James Merrill for the first time in Tucson, in 1987. In December 1986, while he was still working at JNC Communications, Shahid received the prestigious Ingram Merrill Fellowship, from a private foundation run by James Merrill, for *The Half-Inch Himalayas*. In a few months, he heard that Merrill was coming to Tucson for a reading at the University of Arizona Poetry Center. Shahid called the director, Lois Shelton, and told her that he wanted to be a part of each event where Merrill was invited, barring the visit to Desert Museum, where Shelton took everyone (Shahid hated museums). By this time, Shahid had gained a reputation in the city as a wonderful cook. In his own words, his 'cuisine had become quite a legend in Tucson among all kinds of people and I was known for throwing the most extravagant dinners, far more extravagant than anyone'.[2]

According to his friends, he was a brilliant cook. Food was an integral part of his life. It was at Hindu College that Shahid started mastering certain styles of cooking, like Muslim food from Uttar Pradesh, Kashmiri Brahmin food, dishes like rogan josh, yakhni and rajma. Shahid once told his friend Aman Nath that he was never interested in the 'cooking business' as a kid, but when he eventually started cooking, it stayed with him forever.[3] Even during his last years, when he could no longer cook, he made sure that the food that was being prepared by Iqbal, for the friends who had come to see him, had the same taste and flavour. A story that is often recounted with reference to Shahid's cooking is that once he misjudged the number of guests who were coming over for dinner and added extra chilli powder in the main course so people wouldn't ask for seconds.[4]

When Shelton asked him to prepare dinner at her place, Shahid cooked a Kashmiri–Brahmin meal, which received a round of applause from everyone. Merrill had come to Tucson with his new lover, Peter Hooten. At dinner, Shahid asked him if he had been on the panel for the Ingram Merrill Fellowship. Although Merrill didn't reveal it to Shahid at the time, he had an active part in the selection committee and knew Shahid's work. At the party, they talked about the McCarran–Walter Act on citizenship for immigrants of Asian descent, and the Greek poet Yannis Ritsos, who, like Merrill, with his 560-page epic poem 'The Changing Light at Sandover', had also written an epic called 'Epitaphios' and had been an influential figure for Shahid. Merrill congratulated Shahid for *The Half-Inch Himalayas* and said: 'When you come to New York you must get in touch and come to the City and visit us.'[5] In an unpublished essay, Shahid recalled the events of the evening and wrote that 'it was a very enchanting evening. There was a touch about it that placed it above the regular. It seemed there was a lot of elegance to the air because of his presence.'[6]

Illustration 14: Shahid with James Merrill in Tucson, Arizona, 1987.

James Merrill was born to a wealthy family from New York and had a private governess who taught him French and German. In 1944, he was drafted into the United States Army for eight months, but upon his return he joined Amherst College. His thesis was on the work of Marcel Proust, and after his English professor read the thesis, he said that 'he was destined for some sort of greatness'.[7] So he was. Merrill was awarded almost all the literary prizes in America. Harold Bloom had commented on Merrill's *The Book of Ephraim* and said that it rivalled Yeats's *A Vision*. However, it wasn't the epic scale of Merrill's poetry that had caught Shahid's attention but the formalist nature of his works.

Although Merrill himself had written numerous poems in free verse, he had shifted to formal poetry because it offered him more space to function, to discover the hidden secrets of language. But his background and upbringing had led him to a different way of dealing with poetry. All his works had an autobiographical touch that stemmed from loss and nostalgia, much like Proust's works, which Merrill had internalized right before the publication of his first book of poems *The Black Swan*. Shahid, as always, had pointed out the lack of politics in Merrill's poetry, while Merrill, on the other hand, pointed out the lack of formalism in Shahid's works. But Shahid was beginning to understand the ways of formal poetry and writing ghazals in English after having embarked on his translations of Faiz. Shahid saw something in Merrill which he had seen in people such as Mohammad Mujeeb and Begum Akhtar, and thus, he started to write to him. Eventually, a friendship was established, and Shahid started to meet him as much as he could. In *James Merrill: Life and Art*, Langdon Hammer, Merrill's biographer, wrote about Shahid:

> Shahid Ali was another friend important at this time. Merrill and Hooten drove to see him in Amherst, where he was teaching at UMass. As usual, Ali cooked for them an 'amazing' meal, which left Jimmy charmed and Peter, who 'goes for the hot dishes,' bright with sweat. Since meeting Merrill around 1990, Ali had absorbed his work, and changed his own work as a result of it, making a conversion from free verse to intricate formal patterns like the canzone. He was already the author of six poetry collections that meditated on his past in distant, war-torn Kashmir and his dislocated sense of life in the U.S.[8]

Merrill had a massive influence on Shahid's poetry and on the way in which the latter dealt with language. He opened up new avenues for Shahid, and both of them would spend hours breaking down a single stanza of a poem. In one of his interviews, Shahid said, 'Merrill had vetoed certain rhymes: "seem" and "scene" were not acceptable, but "clean" and "scene" were a good pair. And then he said, "Do you have a rhyming dictionary? No? I'll send you one." And I said, "Send me the rhyming dictionary." I revised the poem according to his strictures and he called me to congratulate me about the rhymes I had.'[9] The rhyming dictionary would stay with him forever, and Shahid would make sure that each of his students at Hamilton, at UMass and later at New York University had their rhyming dictionaries with them, because he had come to believe, thanks to Merrill, that it was essential for a poet to hold his language in his hands, to have their own vocabulary which was palpable.

Sameetah, Shahid's youngest sister, remembers one occasion when she, one of her friends and Shahid visited Merrill at his summer home in Stonington, which she described as a huge countryside colonial with stone walls and a sprawling orchard. Throughout the visit, Merrill and Shahid discussed a poem and the choice of words, what effect they had and what they added to the poem. They spent hours breaking down each line, each word, attempting to replace the words to see what that would do to the poem. Eventually, when they left, Sameetah's friend, who had nothing to do with poetry, commented that she had thought poetry was supposed to be something written on the spur of the moment and that after hearing them speak, she realized how much effort went into each poem.[10]

Illustration 15: Shahid with his sister Sameetah, Hamilton College, Clinton, New York, 1989.

Reading Merrill's poetry, Shahid started to understand his own sense of loss. He started to develop an understanding of how a loss of the magnitude that he had experienced right after the death of Begum Akhtar could consume page after page of verse. In a letter to Merrill dated 30 September 1990, Shahid wrote:

> I simply must tell you now when I write I am constantly aware of you. It isn't that I am imitating you (who could?) but that I am trying to learn from you. And strangely enough, my interest in being recognizably formal is proving to be liberating (now I can see many vers-librettos going crazy over this remark). I think free verse in the past two decades has become an exercise in laziness; I still love free verse but I don't see its current practitioners challenging themselves.[11]

Eliot, Faiz and Dickinson had, till this time, been the driving force behind Shahid's poetry. Since he knew the works of Eliot well, Shahid used Eliot's deathly motifs in his poems and learnt the art of intertextuality from him. Dickinson was another figure whose influence Shahid could never escape; he learnt much from her poetry and her ideas about the evanescent. But Merrill was the first person alive whom Shahid had chosen as a mentor and who had a major influence on Shahid's works. And Shahid made the most out of it. He spent a lot of time with Merrill discussing poetry. He cooked for him as well as for Merrill's partner, Peter Hooten. Shahid once said about Merrill: 'I value him immensely as a presence in my work, and I would say he's in some ways the formal spirit guiding me through *The Country without a Post Office*.'[12] In turn, Merrill once told him that Shahid's friendship was important to him and Peter as Shahid was someone who had no sense of Merrill's past with David Jackson, Merrill's former lover, and so they could create a friendship which was unencumbered.[13]

In all his collections published after he became friends with Merrill, Shahid's poems are alive with Merrill's influence as well as his words. 'Feel the patient's heart—pounding—oh please! This once,' reads one of the epigraphs of a ghazal from *Rooms Are Never Finished*. And in his poem 'I Dream I Am at the Ghat of the Only World', Shahid makes a direct reference to Merrill's poem 'The Changing Light at Sandover', evoking Merrill himself in the first stanza: 'Which mirror opened to JM's descent to the skeletoned dark.'[14] He ends the poem with a line borrowed from Merrill's 'For Proust', beckoning Merrill to console him: 'HUSH, SHAHID, THIS IS ME, JAMES, THE LOVED ONE ALWAYS LEAVES.'

By that time, Shahid had started teaching poetry, and so, in class, he would urge his students to read Merrill's poem 'Charles on Fire'. Often, while discussing other matters with Merrill, Shahid would casually slip in a line or a few words from Merrill's poetry, and upon realizing that they were his words, Merrill would gently smile—Shahid's sense of humour was another reason why Merrill liked him.

Merrill and Shahid had once gone to a fancy butcher's shop to buy meat. Shahid insisted that the butcher cut the meat with the bones in. But the butcher kept reminding Shahid that he had to be careful with this and that a child could choke on a bone while eating. To this, Shahid responded saying that he didn't care 'if all the children at the party choked on a bone and died', just to shut him up. Merrill later told him that he often remembered that moment and laughed, saying that it was a pure example of style.[15]

Shahid also developed a taste for other poetic forms that he came in contact with after meeting Merrill. Having come under Merrill's sway, Shahid started to question his allegiance to free verse and started writing more poems in strict measures such as syllabics and sapphics. As he turned towards formal poetry, writing canzones and villanelles, his primary concern was the ghazal, a form that he could claim familiarity with and which had, according to him, been misinterpreted and misappropriated by American poets. He realized that such forms offered more possibilities whereby a writer could find himself or herself 'tantalizingly liberated'.[16] The possibilities offered by formal poetry led him to believe that this was one way in which he could clearly establish his voice while containing his emotion. The three canzones Shahid wrote were about issues that were deeply personal to him: Kashmir, his mother's death and his own imminent death.

On 9 December 1994, Shahid met Merrill in New York, and they spent the day together. First, they had lunch at Merrill's place, where both of them talked about a canzone that Shahid had written (Merrill said that he wished it was consistently pentameter or consistently decasyllabic, and asked Shahid to work on it some more). Later, both went to the Guggenheim Museum, where W.S. Merwin was reading. Merwin and Merrill asked Shahid to come with them to a party where Galway Kinnell and other poets were present. At the party, Shahid watched from a distance as Merrill waved him goodbye, took the elevator and left. To Shahid, he looked tired. That was when Shahid realized that Merrill's health was failing. Shahid went downstairs looking for Merrill, and said goodbye to Merwin and his wife Paula, but Merrill was no longer there. Shahid didn't know it then, but that would be the last time he would see Merrill. On 6 February 1995, Merrill died from complications of AIDS in Tucson.[17] Shahid continued to teach his poems, and although Merrill was no more, he remained with Shahid as a formal spirit.

THIRTEEN

The Cry of the Gazelle

Shahid opened his essay 'The Ghazal in America: May I?' with a demand as well as an accusation: 'I will take back the gift outright: The Americans have got it quite wrong.' In the essay, he narrated an incident from a writers' conference where an American woman kept saying to him, 'Oh, I just love ghazaaals, I'm going to write a lot of ghazaaals', and how, in utter pain, he wanted to say, 'OH PLEASE DON'T.'[1] In the essay, he took issue with the way Americans pronounced the word 'ghazal': 'First, to be petty, the pronunciation. It's pronounced ghuzzle, the gh sounding like a cousin to the French r, the sound excavated near unnoticeably from deep in the throat.'[2] Shahid understood the form of the ghazal, its lyrical capacity and how it functioned. He was irked by the misreading of the form by American poets when he encountered their free-verse ghazals.

In the late '70s, when Shahid arrived in the United States, he read the translations of Mirza Ghalib's ghazals by American poets like W.S. Merwin and Adrienne Rich in *Ghazals of Ghalib*. In his introduction to *Ghazals of Ghalib*, Aijaz Ahmad remarked, 'In such an enterprise, it is absolutely essential that the finished versions be done by persons who are primarily poets and not necessarily scholars of Urdu. This could, of course, be achieved through collaboration only between an Urdu Writer (in this case, myself) and several gifted American poets who have experience in working with raw, literal versions.' He emphasized that 'translation is approximation' and that 'one translation might capture what another misses'.[3] Ahmad had handed out transliterations and lexical notes of the ghazals to revered American translators and poets like Adrienne Rich, W.S. Merwin, David Ray, Mark Strand and William Hunt. The poets and translators were free to digress from the 'strict accuracy' of the details. They weren't asked to adhere to the formal structure of the ghazal and had freedom to translate the ghazals in free verse.

However, rather than putting out translations of couplets written by Ghalib into English, this ended up producing works that were distorted and nowhere near Ghalib's compositions. Instead of translating, Rich and the others had ended up recreating Ghalib's verses. Although Shahid praised their efforts and wrote that Merwin's versions were 'sometimes spectacular, sometimes magical, sometimes passable—but always interesting', he also felt that 'none of these quite suggested the emotional desperation, however quiet, of the original'.[4]

Even when he started translating Faiz in the '80s, Shahid decided to not touch the ghazals and only work with the *nazm*—poems in free verse. Shahid believed that translating a ghazal took tremendous effort and that without the refrain and all the other formal elements, a translation couldn't carry the ghazal's essence. And it wasn't the translations that irked him but the form used by English poets like Rich, Jim Harrison and others.

Adrienne Rich's translations had such an immense impact on her contemporaries and on herself that she started writing ghazals in English, which were very similar to her translations of Ghalib. For her, a ghazal was a package that had a 'concentrating, gathering, and a cumulative effect'.[5] Following in her footsteps, other poets such as Phyllis Webb and Jim Harrison started writing ghazals in English. The free-verse, or *vers libre*, ghazals that they wrote came to be known as anti-ghazals or meta-ghazals after Webb came out with her collection *Sunday Water: Thirteen Anti-Ghazals* (1982) and *Water and Light: Ghazals and Anti-Ghazals* (1984). Webb's feminist poetry, which also dealt with ontological and philosophical issues, such as life, death and rebirth, blended with her anti-ghazals.

In the preface to *Water and Light: Ghazals and Anti-Ghazals*, Webb wrote, 'As I learnt more about Ghazals, I saw I was actually defying some of the traditional rules, constraints, and pleasure laid down so long ago.'[6] Webb observed that her ghazals focused on 'the particular, the local, the dialectical, the private'.[7] In the midst of these appropriations and misappropriations, Shahid started writing against the free-verse ghazal.

Shahid had attended numerous mushairas in Kashmir and Delhi, and was familiar with the manner in which a poet ought to present a ghazal, how they invoked their name in the last couplet and how the refrain cast a spell on the audience. In his introduction to *Ravishing DisUnities: Real Ghazals In English*, he wrote, 'If one writes in free verse—and one should—to subvert Western civilization, surely one should write in forms to save oneself from Western civilization.'[8] Ghazal writing and all its complexities had perplexed the West for a long time, and Shahid questioned the Western penchant for stylistic and thematic unity. He wrote that when his students 'ask about a poem such as "The Waste Land"—How does it hold together?—I suggest a more compelling approach, a tease: How does it not hold together?'[9]

The couplets in a ghazal, unlike a free verse poem, do not have any thematic unity. The diction, style, the independence of the couplets and, at the same time, the constraining formal framework of the ghazal, might perplex a Western reader encountering the form for the first time. 'While one couplet talks about unrequited love, the other talks about man's separation from god, so how is a ghazal, unlike a western poem, unified? This question, the question of unity has forever haunted the westerner trying to understand the ghazal,' Shahid wrote.[10] Although there was thematic disunity in the ghazal, there existed a formal unity, which he explained in the introduction to *Ravishing DisUnities*:

> The opening couplet (called *matla*) sets up a scheme (of rhyme— called *qafia*; and refrain— called *radif*) by having it occur in both lines—the rhyme immediately preceding the refrain—and then this scheme occurs only in the second line of each succeeding couplet. That is, once a poet establishes the scheme—with total freedom, I might add—she or he becomes its slave. What results in the rest of the poem is the alluring tension of a slave trying to master the master. A ghazal has five couplets at least; there is no maximum limit . . . to mark the end of the ghazal, often a poet has a signature couplet (*makhta*) in which s/he can invoke his/her name pseudonymously or otherwise.[11]

'The actual form, by its very nature, erases that expectation [of thematic unity], pre-empts it,' Shahid wrote.[12] He explained how each couplet is independent yet, at the same time, a part of the ghazal, and compared the form to a necklace, where each couplet was a pearl that could shine in isolation, while at the same time form a beautiful necklace. He pointed out that like many other traditions, the ghazal had an oral purpose and was sung by singers like Begum Akhtar; that it was the ghazal's formal unity, metre, rhyme and refrain, as well as the anticipation, that saved it from arbitrariness. The ghazal was meant to be presented at mushairas, where the poet would recite the first couplet and establish the refrain. The people in the audience, who were aware of the refrain, would wait in anticipation for the poet to enthral them with wordplay, and they would applaud and 'wah-wah' in rapture. This back and forth, the tension created by the refrain, the anticipation of the next couplet and the familiarity with the end rhyme, was what held a ghazal together. All of this had allowed tragic poets such as Ghalib to reveal their emotions in a comprehensive—or what a Westerner might call disjointed—manner.

Shahid had written that he didn't want to come across as a 'rheumatic formalist', but he believed that if American poets understood the niceties of ghazals, they could work wonders. According to him, few understood the true meaning of form, one of whom was the poet John Hollander. On 1 October 1994, Shahid wrote a letter to Hollander, who—although Shahid had his reservations about it—he believed was the closest that any American poet had reached to mastering the form. He began the letter with: 'May I quarrel with you a bit, even though you don't know me?' He stressed that he loved Hollander's ghazal in *Rhyme's Reason* but continued to make a case against his version, stating that there were formal demands that Hollander hadn't met, to which the latter replied, 'I'm most grateful for the corrections.'[13]

By the mid-'90s, Shahid tried to create a larger understanding of the ghazal form through an anthology, later published as *Ravishing DisUnities*. He asked various poets, including Marilyn Hacker, John Hollander and others, to contribute to it. By this time, he had also started writing ghazals in English, explaining the form to the West while exploring his own concerns in a familiar form. Within a decade, the ghazal had gained a reputation in America, and Shahid's ghazals turned into the examples through which others could learn. Perhaps one of his most famous—if not the best—ghazals is 'Tonight', where the force that holds the poem together is Shahid's amalgamation of different concerns:

Where are you now? Who lies beneath your spell tonight?
Whom else from rapture's road will you expel tonight?

Those 'Fabrics of Cashmere—' 'to make Me beautiful—'
'Trinket'—to gem—'Me to adorn—How tell'—tonight?

I beg for haven: Prisons, let open your gates—
A refugee from Belief seeks a cell tonight.

. . . And I, Shahid, only am escaped to tell thee—
God sobs in my arms. Call me Ishmael tonight.[14]

The word 'Tonight' acts as the radif and is repeated throughout the ghazal, while all the words rhyming with 'spell' and 'expel' act as the qafia or the end rhyme. 'Tonight' follows every rule of what Shahid deemed 'the real thing', the Persian form of the ghazal, similar to any ghazal written in the Indian subcontinent.

While Shahid uses mannerisms of American poetry and culture, and makes references to various poets such as Emily Dickinson, Oscar Wilde, James Merrill and W.H. Auden, he also stays true to the form's essence or its ghazal-ness. In *Ravishing DisUnities*, he wrote, 'The ghazal is not an occasion for angst; it is an occasion for grief.' In Shahid's ghazals, there is desire for the beloved and the pain of separation, there is fatalism and there is hope, there is god and there is separation from god.[15] While on the one hand he borrowed from Rilke and Eliot, he also evoked Ghalib and Faiz, and transformed the manner in which American poets approached the ghazal.

Shahid spent years reworking his ghazals, trying to get as close to the original as possible, and in doing so, he transformed the manner in which America viewed the form. In *Call Me Ishmael Tonight*, the ghazal with the refrain 'Arabic' (originally published in *The Country without a Post Office*) and the ghazal 'In Arabic' (a reworking of the same ghazal), both are present.[16] Not only can one see how the ghazal became stronger over time but also how his concerns became widened politically and emotionally. The couplet 'I too, Oh Amichai, saw the dresses of beautiful women. / And everything else, just like you, in Death, Hebrew, and Arabic', transformed over time into 'I too, O Amichai, saw everything, just like you did– / In Death. In Hebrew. And (please let me stress) in Arabic', where the radif (refrain) became 'in Arabic' from 'Arabic'. In the new version Shahid also included 'stress'—the qafia (rhyme) missing from the previous version—which rhymes with 'Yes', 'caress', and 'less' from the preceding couplets. Not only did he bring out the true form of the ghazal, he also added a political weight to the couplet with the choice of words.

While Shahid admired minimalist American poetry, he belonged to a very different lineage of poets. He had grown up listening to Urdu poetry, quite expansive in its metaphors as compared to American poetry. The metaphors in an Urdu ghazal are never simple—the pain of separation is compared to the end of the world, the beloved's gaze pierces the heart—and are always amplified to create a certain effect. This magnification of loss or nostalgia through the metaphor had been present in Shahid's poetry all along. In 'Tonight', he wrote, 'Call me Ishmael tonight', which may seem like a reference to the opening line of Herman Melville's *Moby Dick* but is also a reference to the story of Ishmael's sacrifice that his mother had narrated to him. In the story from the Koran, unlike the version in the Bible, God demands that Abraham sacrifice his son Ishmael as a test, and when Abraham informs Ishmael of this demand, he agrees to be sacrificed. Sufia often said that 'if God had anything to be embarrassed about, it had to be this demand'.[17]

The ghazal's existence in two worlds, geographies and cultures turned the form into a comfortable space for Shahid, where he could be truly expressive. In his ghazals, he emerges as a mystic who interprets the world in a very different manner from a modern poet. In 'From the Start', Shahid sympathizes with Satan and calls him the arch-lover who was exiled when God asked him to bow down to God's new lover, Adam—a belief that resonates with that of Sufi saints, who viewed Satan in a similar fashion.

In other ghazals, Shahid presented himself as a master of wordplay. Once Derek Walcott asked Shahid the meaning of his name, and he said it meant 'beloved' in Persian and 'witness' in Arabic. Later, Shahid admitted that these two things were central to his poetry: the act of witnessing and that of being the beloved. 'As beloved, it means having been in love and having been loved, and having found a lot of satisfaction and fullness through it. As witness, I know there has always been a political element in my life.'[18] Placing his name as the *takhallus* (a pseudonym that a poet uses in the last couplet of a ghazal), in his ghazal 'In Arabic', Shahid writes:

> They ask me to tell them what *Shahid* means: Listen, listen:
> It means 'The Beloved' in Persian, 'witness' in Arabic.[19]

Shahid followed a magpie method, assembling phrases, read or heard, in his poems. This was the case with most of his ghazals, for which he would often borrow lines from other people's poems. When he read the line by E.E. Cummings 'nobody, not even the rain, has such small hands', he ended up using it in his ghazal 'Even the Rain'. Once, Christopher Merrill was taking care of W.S. Merwin's place in Maui, which Shahid and he referred to as 'the Promised Land'. As Christopher Merrill wrote in his book *Self-Portrait with Dogwood*, 'One day, brewing a cup of tea during a long phone conversation with him and finding only honey to sweeten it, I intoned, "There is no sugar in the Promised Land." He seized on the poetic potential of my joke, and we laughed like mad men playing around with lines to close the couplet. The refrain we came up with—"Swear by the olive in the God-kissed land"—was not a perfect rhyme, which pleased him all the more.'[20]

Although this intertextuality—a term coined by Julia Kristeva in the '70s—was a result of his reading of Western poets, it was an integral part of the tradition of ghazals, where poets would use lines of their precursors and, at times, even of their contemporaries. Shahid had reworked Eliot's maxim 'immature poets imitate; mature poets steal' and had extended it to 'Read ravenously and be interested in being influenced'. He had learnt how to incorporate allusions into the fabric of his poetry. 'Will the reader get it or not?' he once said in an interview. 'If they get it that's great, it's wonderful. I am a bit of a conservative or an elitist in this matter. If people are serious about poetry, they should know their Shakespeare, they should know their Milton. They should be devouring poetry all the time, and some of the pleasure is in recognizing.'[21]

Shahid came from the Urdu–Persian tradition, and the idea of 'stealing' the words of other poets was nothing new for him. 'Something can trigger it off any time and I will just go and jot things down,' he explained in an interview. 'A phrase will occur somewhere, either spontaneously or someone will say something, a chance thing, and I'll say, ah, that can lead to a poem. Then I try to find time when I can be alone and work on the poem. Phrases such as this would often lead to a poem.'[22] Shahid was always on the lookout for a phrase or a line, jotting everything down and trying to make it work in a stanza, and he wrote some 'willed poems' as well. But he also believed that 'the subject must happen to a poem, not be forced upon it'.[23]

When finally Shahid took hold of the ghazal, or rather the ghazal took hold of him, it changed everything. Writing ghazals in English allowed him to express all his concerns as an immigrant in America and his hyphenated experience. It brought him closer to what he knew, to his home, the traditions that had shaped him, and it brought him closer to himself. Shahid believed that he had dual loyalties and that they had to lend to each other until they coalesced in a manner which represented all the cultures he belonged to. Thus, gradually, as he became more aware of those loyalties and came to understand—through his friendship with

James Merrill—all that formal poetry could do, he began writing ghazals in English. Shahid, being a transnational writer, merged two different world views together.

These ghazals, over time, took on an identity of their own, different from the Persian ghazal that existed outside the realm of American poetry. It is true that the ghazals Shahid wrote, and those that others wrote following him, weren't a replica of the ghazal in Urdu or Persian. Naturally, there were disparities, and it would have been a shame if the form had not taken on a new identity in a new language. As the French proverb goes, *plus ça change plus c'est la même chose* (the more it changes, the more it remains the same). And in Shahid's hands, the ghazal was renewed while remaining true to its essence, transforming the way the form was viewed and perceived in America.

FOURTEEN

Kashmir, Kaschmir, Cashmere

In 1993, after a spell of six years at Hamilton College, Shahid was offered the position of director of the MFA programme at the University of Massachusetts and moved to Amherst. In the early '90s, Amherst was a cultural space that numerous writers and poets inhabited. It was here that Shahid became friends with Edward Said and Eqbal Ahmad, although they had been acquaintances and had met before. In March 1989, the three of them, along with Akeel Bilgrami and Ibrahim Abu-Lughod, submitted a joint statement to the editor of the *New York Review of Books* condemning the attack on Salman Rushdie following the publication of *The Satanic Verses* and the fatwa issued against him:

As writers and scholars from the Islamic world we are appalled by the vilification, book banning and threats of physical violence against Salman Rushdie, the gifted author of *Midnight's Children*, *Shame*, and *The Satanic Verses*. This campaign is done in the name of Islam, although none of it does Islam any credit. Certainly Muslims and others are entitled to protest against *The Satanic Verses* if they feel the novel offends their religion and cultural sensibilities. But to carry protest and debate over into the realm of bigoted violence is in fact antithetical to Islamic traditions of learning and tolerance. We deplore and regret this sort of thing, and we reaffirm our belief in universal principles of rational discussion and freedom of expression.[1]

The three of them shared a love of Urdu poetry and were committed to anti-war politics—they never refrained from pointing out American hypocrisies. Shahid once told Saleem Kidwai a story about Edward Said, who called Shahid one day and said that he had good as well as bad news, and asked him what he would like to hear first. 'Shahid asked for the bad news. Said told him that Aijaz Ahmad [the Marxist literary theorist whose book *In Theory* was as popular as it was reviled] had had a heart attack. The good news, Said added, was that it had happened in England, where the health services are really bad.'[2] It was at Amherst that Said asked Shahid to translate the poetry of Mahmoud Darwish, even though Shahid couldn't read Arabic. Thus, along with Ahmad Dalal, an Arabic translator, Shahid translated Darwish's poems and published them as part of series entitled *Eleven Stars Over Andalusia*. Though Said and Shahid were friends, the latter was much closer to Eqbal Ahmad, who came over to Shahid's house for dinners regularly to talk about politics, war, poetry, literature and Kashmir.

Shahid, as usual, would host dinner parties where students, professors, writers and others would gather. Ahmad was among the few people who were always at Shahid's place. In the '70s, Ahmad had been exiled by the Pakistani government and had found refuge in Beirut, where he came in touch with Edward Said. It was Ahmad who had introduced Faiz to Said. Recounting his time with Faiz in Beirut, Ahmad said in an interview with David Barisman:

I think it was 1980. Zia-ul Haq was the military dictator in Pakistan . . . He [Faiz Ahmad Faiz] came to my lecture in Beirut. I noticed him sitting in the back. I went up to him and introduced him to Edward . . . At one point, we were having dinner in a restaurant where curfew had already been imposed but we continued to stay on and fighting had begun. Faiz recited several poems as I translated them verbatim. We all ignored the shooting and went on.[3]

Illustration 16: Shahid in 1997. Photograph taken by Neil Davenport.

It was their love for Faiz that brought Shahid and Ahmad together. Ahmad would later speak of the power of Urdu poetry stating that at a bilingual reading with Shahid (where Ahmad read the Urdu originals and Shahid read his translations) 'a lot of Americans who know nothing of Urdu had tears in their eyes'.[4] Until his death in 1999, Ahmad visited Shahid regularly and, according to Iqbal, 'they discussed everything under the sun'.[5] Shahid once said: 'Whenever we talked to Eqbal about anybody on the earth, he seemed to have met that person. So we talked about Malcolm X, and he would say: "Oh Malcolm!" Louis Ferrier, "Oh Louis!" So I asked my mother what if I mentioned Prophet Mohammed to him. She said that Eqbal would say, "I was the scribe who took down the Koran."'[6]

Amherst was special for Shahid, for it was the birthplace as well as the resting place of Emily Dickinson, a poet Shahid greatly admired. In *A Nostalgist's Map of America*, published a year before he moved to Amherst, he had borrowed extensively from Dickinson. When Shahid moved to Amherst, he realized that Dickinson had made several references to 'Cashmere' in her poems. 'As soon as I realized that there were six times Dickinson had used Kashmir in her poems, I quickly used them in my poems before anyone else could,' Shahid said at the farewell event for Eqbal Ahmad at New Hampshire College in 1997.[7] However, by the time Shahid was in Amherst, Kashmir had already turned into *cauchemar*—the French word for nightmare.

The Kashmiri struggle for self-determination was at its peak in the '90s, and an intifada-style militancy had risen in the Valley. The Indian government had responded by sending in troops, which resulted in further tensions. On 21 January 1990, a peaceful protest on the Gawkadal bridge in Srinagar was disrupted by paramilitary forces, who shot at the protesters and killed fifty-two people.[8] 'The paramilitaries surrounded unarmed demonstrators on the bridge and indiscriminately shot at them with automatic rifles,' the novelist Mirza Waheed wrote in *Time* magazine, recollecting the events of the day. 'They then poked the piled-up bodies on the bridge to check if anyone was alive.'⁹ This moment, according to many, marked the beginning of the armed conflict in Kashmir.

Although the Kashmir crisis flared up in the '90s, the seeds of the conflict were sown around the time of Partition. On 16 March 1846, Maharaja Gulab Singh, a Dogra ruler, signed the Treaty of Amritsar and bought Kashmir from the British for a sum of 75 lakh Nanak Shahi rupees, thus establishing Dogra rule in the Valley.[10] In 1947, Kashmir was under the rule of Maharaja Hari Singh, the Hindu ruler of a predominantly Muslim majority state. Even during his rule, he faced backlash from the Muslim population of the state. By the mid-'40s, Sheikh Abdullah had gained prominence, and on 20 May 1946, he launched the Quit Kashmir movement and was subsequently imprisoned for three years.[11] However, the Dogra rule in Kashmir soon began to feel the tremors of the Indian independence struggle. When the British Raj came to an end in August 1947 and the nation partitioned, Maharaja Hari Singh was torn and couldn't decide which side to lean on.

By 21 October, the Pakistan Army, along with Pashtun tribal invaders, entered Kashmir. Within five days, the maharaja, in a state of panic, acceded to India and signed the Instrument of Accession.[12] During the course of the next few months, in 1947–48, India and Pakistan fought their first war, and India referred the Kashmir dispute to the United Nations. In 1948, the United Nations declared that after Pakistan had removed its troops, India would do the same and a plebiscite would be held in the state to decide their future. When ceasefire was agreed upon in 1949, India held 65 per cent of the region, while the rest was under the control of Pakistan.[13] Sheikh Abdullah, one of the major leaders of Kashmir, was appointed as the prime minister of the state in 1947. Abdullah was close to Nehru. However, according to the political commentator A.G. Noorani, Abdullah's Kashmiri nationalism clashed with Nehru's Indian nationalism. 'The clash was inherent even at the best of times,'

Noorani wrote. This divide led to Abdullah's arrest in 1953 following the Kashmir conspiracy case.[14]

In 1957, the Jammu and Kashmir constituent assembly was dissolved, and the state held its first legislative elections and was fully integrated into India. By 1965, the title of *sard-i-riyasat* (prime minister) was officially changed to chief minister. One year later, the Kashmiri people demanded the promised referendum, and several armed outfits, such as the Jammu and Kashmir Liberation Front (JKLF), emerged.[15] Over the next two decades, there was a rise in the number of militant outfits in the state as well in the number of arrests and killings of the militant youth. Throughout the '90s, all protests were dealt with in a similar fashion. There were army checkposts at each street corner, and the draconian Armed Forces Special Powers Act, popularly known as AFSPA, which gave the armed forces complete immunity, was imposed.

According to the political scientist Sumantra Bose, 'Between 1990 and 1994, the peak of the armed struggle, 5119 were killed and thousands more captured.'[16] It was a time when all resistance was crushed using oppression, torture and fear, when protestors were met with brute force, when the paradise on earth turned into a paradise lost. Although the chants of 'azadi' (freedom) could be heard all around the Valley, there was also the deafening sound of gunfire and explosives. The Association of Parents of Disappeared Persons (APDP), an organization that was founded in 1994 to help the family members of missing persons in the region, claims that between 8000 to 10,000 people have gone missing as a result of the 'enforced disappearances'.[17]

In 2011, over 2700 unmarked graves were identified in four districts of Kashmir by an eleven-member police team of the State Human Rights Commission. Out of the 2700 graves, 574 bodies were identified as those of 'disappeared locals'. As for the remaining 2100 unidentified graves, the police report concluded that they 'may contain the dead bodies of [the victims of] enforced disappearances'.[18] The violence, oppression and human rights violations that began in the '90s have continued in Kashmir, and the conflict has since claimed 70,000 lives.[19] 'Normalcy, normalcy,' Shahid had written in an unfinished essay. 'It sounds obscene when one realizes it is built on seventy thousand corpses. The peace of the graveyard, the normalcy death gives way to.'[20]

FIFTEEN

Crimsoned Spillages

For almost a decade, Shahid hadn't used the word 'Kashmir' in his poetry. As he was chasing the evanescent landscapes of Tucson, transforming the ghazal and exploring his hyphenated identity, Kashmir, somehow, had fallen into the backdrop. However, when he finally uttered the word in his seminal collection *The Country without a Post Office*, he launched into a frenzy, repeating it over and over and over, allowing it to spiral through a web of semantic associations. Shahid broke into a refrain—like King Lear, who shouted 'never, never, never, never, never, never' after Cordelia's death; or like Walt Whitman's 'Death, Death, Death, Death' in 'Out of the Cradle Endlessly Rocking'—and entered a sphere where words turned into sounds, losing (or gaining?) all meaning. 'Kashmir' turned into an incantation, a spell whereby Shahid lay the word flat in front of himself to reinvent 'an imaginary homeland, filling it, closing it, shutting himself (myself in it)':

> Let me cry out in that void, say it as I can. I write on that void:
> Kashmir, Kaschmir, Cashmere, Qashmir, Cashmir, Cashmire,
> Kashmere, Cachemire, Cushmeer, Cachmiere, Cašmir.
> Or Cauchemar in a sea of stories? Or: Kacmir,
> Kaschemir, Kasmere, Kachmire, Kasmir. Kerseymere?[1]

Before the situation turned gruesome in Kashmir in the '90s, Shahid had spent three summers in the Valley. Each summer, he would visit his home in Rajbagh and then return to New York, where he was teaching at Hamilton College. For that brief period, he had taken both places, both homes for granted. But questions such as 'Will this be the last time I go there?' had started haunting him.[2] As things developed in Kashmir, so did the meaning of the word 'Kashmir' for Shahid. With time, it had acquired new meanings, and from being a metaphor for home, it had turned into a metaphor for a lost homeland.

Shahid was distraught with what Kashmir had turned into, and the violence deeply affected him. In the past, he had responded by writing poems whenever he heard or read about an act of injustice. In many ways, he was a poet of injustice, like Faiz Ahmad Faiz, Yannis Ritsos and César Vallejo. But Shahid was also like Paul Celan, a poet of witness—one who bore testimony to the violence and plight his homeland and its people were going through. He not only wrote poems condemning acts that he believed were unjust, but also wrote essays in journals, bringing history to the forefront.

Shahid was always interested in matters 'of political conscience and of fairness', and admitted that his poetry was politically informed. Yet, he was of the view that he wasn't a political poet.[3] No matter what he wrote, Shahid never wanted to act as a mouthpiece. Amitav Ghosh remarked to him, some time before his death, that he was 'the closest that Kashmir had to a national poet', to which Shahid had replied, 'A national poet, maybe. But not a nationalist poet, please not that.'[4] He had been simply moved by injustice ever since he was a kid. He once said in an interview, 'Events like the Armenian massacre bring out a rage in me. So inadvertently I might be doing some representing. But I don't *represent*, never offer *the* correct version of history.'[5]

As a poet, Shahid had come to the conclusion that it wasn't the subject matter but how the subject was expressed which held more importance. In one of his essays, he argued if all the poems about the Holocaust were essentially the same. He once stated that there were times when he would 'forgive' poems because he liked their compassion and agreed with their politics, and that it took him a while to realize that good politics wasn't the same as good poetry. Later, in an interview, he said that 'subject matter is artistically interesting only when through form it has become content. The more rigorous the form, realized formally, openly, or brokenly, the greater the chance for content.'[6] This was one of the reasons that *The Country without a Post Office* turned into a seminal book that offered a peek into the crisis in Kashmir and cemented Shahid's position as one of the most lyrical poets from the subcontinent.

When the insurgency in Kashmir was at its height in the '90s and the crackdowns began, the postal services in the Valley were shut down. Heaps of undelivered letters littered the post offices as no mail was delivered. One day, as Shahid's friend Irfan Hasan entered an abandoned post office, he found a letter lying on the floor, addressed to Agha Ashraf Ali. He delivered the letter himself and narrated the incident to Shahid, which immediately led him to the phrase 'Country without a Post Office'.[7] In an essay, Shahid wrote that he had vivid dreams about the undelivered letters. While narrating one such dream, he asked, 'Will they [his letters] reach the forlorn ghosts forlorn for me?'[8] The sight struck him so much that Shahid ended up writing the first draft of the poem, which eventually led to a collection that would shape Kashmiri resistance literature for decades.

In Shahid's verses, Srinagar, his muse, is a 'city from where no news can come'. Glimpses of the city he grew up in, the place he knew best, can be seen throughout the collection. In Srinagar, one can trace Shahid's footsteps from Mir Pan House on Residency

Road to Gupkar Road and the Cantonment. On these streets, he followed the 'crimsoned spillages'. In Shahid's depiction of the suffering of the people, the physical body is an important part. The 'webs of hands' are 'cut with a knife', hands blossom into fists, hands carry gods in their arms. It is the body that is tortured—on which drippings from a burning tyre fall—and that remains unburied. Although the bodies are tormented, something much deeper is crushed by the pain, and so, at times, the flesh and bone are absent in his verses. Only the shadows, chased by searchlights looking for the bodies, are left to console the poet. And Shahid, like other forlorn ghosts of the Valley, is left alone.

There is a strange feeling of helplessness that emerges from Shahid's verses. This helpless resignation is reminiscent of Paul Celan's misery—Celan's father died in a concentration camp, and his mother was shot in the neck by the Nazis—when he wrote, in 'Ashglory', 'no one / bears witness for / the witness'. Although there are self-referential elements in Shahid's poetry which are veiled by metaphors, there is a sense of openness in his verse, encompassing the concerns of the whole Kashmiri society.

When Shahid showed an early draft of his poem 'The Correspondent' to James Merrill, the latter called him out for his 'irresponsible rhymes'. Merrill said to him, '. . . in these terminal seasons of human artistry we must be careful never to rhyme "seem" and "scene." If it's "scene," it should be "clean," but not "seem".'[9] Eventually, in 'The Correspondent', a poem that follows a rhyme scheme for seven stanzas, Shahid rhymed 'scene' with 'damascene' and 'sheen' among other words, but heeded Merrill's advice and left out 'seem':

I say, 'There's no way back to your country,'
I tell him he must never leave. He cites
the world: his schedule. I set up barricades:
the mountain routes are damp;

there, dead dervishes damascene
the dark. 'I must leave now,' his voice ablaze.
I take off—it's my last resort—my shadow.

And he walks—there's no electricity—
back into my dark, murmurs Kashmir!, lights
(to a soundtrack of exploding grenades)
a dim kerosene lamp.
'We must give back the hour its sheen.
Or this spell will never end . . . Quick,' he says,
'I've just come—with videos—from Sarajevo.'[10]

Although he believed that his political subject matter was not
at odds with his aesthetic philosophy, Shahid was always of the
opinion that the aesthetic must never be sacrificed for the political,
in poetry as well as in life. What eventually turned *The Country
without a Post Office* into an iconic collection was not only its
political subject matter, but also the style in which it was written.
The beauty of *The Country without a Post Office* comes from its
lyrical nature, which owes much to the poems written in forms
like the villanelle ('A Villanelle'), ghazal ('Ghazal') and canzone.
While in a villanelle the same lines recur multiple times—it is, in
the words of Mark Strand, an 'elaborate system of retrievals . . .
[which] does most to suggest recovery'—in a ghazal the refrain
attains new meanings in each couplet, offering, at the same time,
a certain coherence that binds everything together.

It is through such poems, through the repetition of words,
phrases and ideas, that Shahid sheds light on the suffering of the
Kashmiri people. In the pantoum 'Muharram in Srinagar 1992',
Shahid borrows a phrase from Paul Celan's 'Death Fugue'—'Death
is a master from Germany'—and, with reference to the Battle of
Karbala to express his grief at the sight of 'streets in which blood
flows like Husain's', writes about the army's siege of Srinagar in

a charged manner. T.S. Eliot had stated, 'When forced to work within a strict framework the imagination is taxed to its utmost—and will produce its richest ideas. Given total freedom the work is likely to sprawl.'[11] The restrictions of the form forced him to work within the constraints. The result? Verses that turned his grief into epic laments.

Of all his poems about Kashmir, the one that captures the essence of the suffering and pain is the canzone 'After an August Wedding in Lahore'.[12] Like Shahid's two other canzones—'Lenox Hill', written after his mother's death, and 'The Veiled Suite', his final poem—this one works on a lavish scale, assuming the voice of millions and presenting their suffering in a lyrical manner. The question he asks is not whether there will be singing in the dark times—he knows that songs will be sung—but what his voice should lament:

A brigadier says, *The boys of Kashmir*
break so quickly, we make their bodies sing
on the rack, till no song is left to sing.
'Butterflies pause / On their passage Cashmere—'
And happiness: must it only bring pain?
The century is ending. It is pain

from which love departs into all new pain:
Freedom's terrible thirst, flooding Kashmir,
is bringing love to its tormented glass.
Stranger, who will inherit the last night
of the past? Of what shall I not sing, and sing?

It is as though Shahid extended his mourning through punctuation, using periods, commas and dashes to pause and lament. He italicized 'Kashmir' at times, so the slant could represent how fractured the place was. He moved away from writing coherently to bring out the confusion and derangement, and in his language used silences, whispers and brief moments of stillness symbolizing uncertainty.

His poems are elegiac verses that speak directly about the suffering of the Kashmiri people, and he weaved all the elements—atrocities, fear, anger and pain—together to display the pregnant moment as a whole, which not only represented what Kashmir had turned into but also grieved the loss of the other—the Kashmiri Pandits.

In September 1989, Pandit Tika Lal Taploo, president of the Bharatiya Janata Party's Kashmir chapter, was shot dead by masked men. Three weeks later, a retired judge, Nilakanth Ganjoo, was shot in broad daylight.[13] Numerous other killings, of Kashmiri Pandits, followed. 'An important element of the background [of the exodus of Kashmiri Pandits] is also the killing of a number of senior Pandit officials in various organisations,' historian Mridu Rai said in an interview. 'The militants claimed that they were only targeting Indian agents but, from the Pandit perspective, the fact that the targets were exclusively Hindu was an indication that the threat was a communal one.'[14] According to various accounts, announcements were made, from loudspeakers on mosques, asking the Pandits to vacate the Valley and giving them three options: *ralive, tsaliv ya galive* (convert, leave or perish). *Aftab*, a popular Urdu daily, reiterated the same message.[15] Instead of protecting the religious minority, Jagmohan, the governor of Kashmir, announced that if 'the Pandits decided to leave, refugee camps had been set up for them', but if 'they chose to stay back, he would not be able to guarantee their safety'.[16] A fear psychosis followed, and soon, the Pandits were left with no choice but to leave the Valley.

According to the political scientist Alexander Evans, between 1,50,000 and 1,60,000 Kashmiri Pandits left the Valley in 1990.[17] A 2010 report of the Internal Displacement Monitoring Centre of the Norwegian Refugee Council suggests the number is closer to 2,50,000, while another report by the CIA claims that 3,00,000 people were displaced.[18] As the Pandits fled their homeland in search of a safe haven, they left a vacuum in the Valley, a void that deeply disturbed Shahid, and in *The Country without a Post Office*, he spoke of all that he had lost—including the Pandits who, though far away from home, wore 'jeweled ice in dry plains / to will the distant mountains to glass'.[19]

Growing up, Shahid had many friends who were Pandits, and naturally, their exile had a massive impact on him. In fact, Shahid's favourite cuisine was Kashmiri Brahmin food. Not only was this a result of his closeness to Pandits but also of the values he had grown up with. Ashraf had once stated that 'Indian history can never be written impartially and truthfully unless, when we begin to write it, we forget that Aurangzeb was a Muslim and Shivaji a Hindu'. Shahid, and his three siblings, had inherited this ideology, which was inclusive in all aspects. His sense of community was not restricted to Kashmiri Muslims and was, in many ways, the epitome of the idea of Kashmiriyat. It can be sensed in his poem 'Farewell', a lament for the Kashmiri Pandits and a poem that has a curious history.

For a long time, Shahid had been reading language poets, such as Michael Palmer and Jorie Graham, who had been using one-line stanzas. Shahid, as a poet, was envious of their one-line stanzas, as well as those of the Polish poet Czeslaw Milosz. Once, while his friend and colleague Patricia O'Neill was speaking to him on the phone, she had casually uttered a line, 'Your memory is getting into the way of my history.' Shahid picked it up instantly and weaved it into the body of his poem 'Farewell', making the line work in numerous ways: 'Your memory gets in the way of my memory' and 'my memory keeps getting in the way of your history'.[20]

In his poetry, he never dreamt of a utopian Kashmir. His home was a place lost to time, as it was for the Russian poet Osip Mandelstam—when he wrote 'We Shall Meet Again in Petersburg'—whom Shahid evoked in the first poem of *The Country without a Post Office*: 'The Blessed Word: A Prologue'. Published in 1920, six years after Saint Petersburg was renamed to Petrograd, the poem's essence was placed in time, not space. In 'A Guide to a Renamed City', Joseph Brodsky wrote that 'it is with the emergence of St. Petersburg that Russian literature came into existence'.[21] For Mandelstam, and even Anna Akhmatova, the name Petrograd represented all that the city had lost. Shahid, too, had lost his homeland to conflict and wanted to return to a bygone era. Although *The Country without a Post Office* presented Shahid as a poet who sang about the dark times, he was in fact a poet of peace in times of conflict and simply lived, like Mandelstam, 'in the imperative of the future passive participle—in the "what ought to be"'.[22]

Sometime after the publication of *The Country without a Post Office*, the Kashmiri artist Masood Hussain visited Shahid in Srinagar. Sitting in his veranda with his electronic typewriter, Shahid handed him some couplets that he had written and asked him to adapt them into paintings. The couplets, to Hussain's surprise, eulogized the beauty of Kashmir. According to Hussain, 'They presented a contrast from the nature of our works which largely were a testimony to the ongoing turmoil in the Valley.'[23] One of the untitled couplets reads:

What measureless measures, the colors of fire clinging to the chinars, to the reflections of chinars,

to your eyes as from them you see the last grand crimsoned spillage.

Shahid, as Hussain would realize much later, was looking past the ongoing conflict, staring past all that had been lost, already searching for all that could be regained. He was hopeful that peace would come back to the Valley. And why not? After all, even Mandelstam's Petersburg had returned, shaking off a century's worth of ashes, after the fall of the Soviet Union. There always was room for hope, for Shahid to keep the promise he had made to his friend Irfan Hasan, to sing of the promising and not the promised end. However, soon, everything would change, and Kashmir, which had been a metaphor for a lost homeland, would turn into the scale with which he would measure loss.

SIXTEEN

From Amherst to Kashmir

Death had been a recurring theme in Shahid's poetry ever since he was a teenager in Kashmir, reading Eliot's verses. 'He who was living is now dead / We who were living are now dying / With a little patience.'[1] It was a motif that remained with him for the rest of his life. The first two collections he published, *Bone Sculpture* and *In Memory of Begum Akhtar*, both contained the imagery of death. In these collections, death transmutes into a phantasmagoria, revealing evanescing memories and leaving only shadows. Although the dying and the dead, at times, remain invisible, death is a figure that is always present. In 'Cremation', written after the death of his friend Vidur Wazir's mother, the bones of the dead refuse to burn. In the poem 'In Memory of Begum Akhtar', Akhtari's death is in 'every paper, boxed in the black and white of photographs'. Although the passing of figures and friends such as Begum Akhtar and James Merrill had their effect on Shahid, the death of his mother and the outburst that followed is in no manner comparable to the ones that came before.

In the late '70s, when Shahid was a professor at Hindu College, his family had bought him a flat in New Delhi's Zakir Bagh. Even when he had left for America, the family retained the apartment. In the '90s, it became an escape for Ashraf and Sufia from the harsh winters of Kashmir; they spent two to three months each year in New Delhi. In December 1995, at the Zakir Bagh apartment, Sufia had her first seizure. The initial suspicion of the doctors in New Delhi was that it was a tapeworm, but after the diagnosis came through, they found that it was a malignant brain tumour. At that time, Shahid and Iqbal were at Amherst, Hena was completing her PhD at the University of Massachusetts, and Sameetah was a professor of art history at Pratt Institute in New York. When the news of the seizure reached the siblings in America, Iqbal flew to Delhi to bring Sufia to America for treatment. She was admitted to Lenox Hill Hospital in New York, and within two days of her arrival the doctors performed a surgery.

After the surgery, the exhausted Sufia said to Shahid that the sirens of New York traffic sounded like the elephants of Mihiragula. When Shahid asked his father who Mihiragula was, Ashraf told him about the legend of the cruel Hun invader. It is said that around the sixth century CE, the Hun invader Mihiragula was crossing the Pir Panjal mountain range in Kashmir when one of his elephants slipped and fell to its death. Mihiragula allegedly loved the sound of the elephant's shriek so much that he had an entire herd of elephants pushed from the mountains, just so he could hear the sound again and again. The Mihiragula story remained with Shahid, and months after Sufia's death in 1997, he used it in the epigraph to his second canzone, 'Lenox Hill'.

Although tired and ill, Sufia had retained her charisma. Shahid often said that '[Sufia] had the grandeur of a Sufi', that she'd taught him compassion when he was a young boy.[2] He had always felt supported by Sufia, who had stood by him at all times and played an integral, perhaps even the most crucial, role in shaping his identity. Amitav Ghosh, whom Shahid became friends with in Brooklyn, said, 'She was his muse—his moon and his sun. Shahid used to say that his mother looked like Begum Akhtar and would often say that he looked like Begum Akhtar as well: "*Mere bhi daant zara unchain hai. Haina*? (Her teeth were a little prominent, so are mine. No?)'"[3] If Ashraf had contributed to the rational side of Shahid, his mother was responsible for the mystic and Sufi element in his manner of thinking, where dualities weren't pitted against each other but viewed as a natural occurrence. During Sufia's time at Lenox Hill, there was grief and there was hope, but in a few months all that would turn into despair and rage.

At Lenox Hill Hospital in Manhattan, Sufia told Shahid, 'As you sit here by me, you're just like my mother.'[4] He, on the other hand, imagined her as a young bride in Kashmir, watching her first film at Regal Cinema Hall with his father. As he watched her suffer in agony, he wondered: 'How helpless was God's mother!' There were times when he wished that she would die, not because he wanted her to but, as he expressed in the poem, to save her as she was, 'young, in song in Kashmir'. The surgery performed by the doctors at Lenox Hill did more harm than good and resulted in a partial paralysis. The family decided to move her to Iqbal's house in Amherst, where she remained for almost a year, battling the cancer. At the approach of dawn on 24 April 1997, Sufia drew her last breath at a hospital in Northampton.

She meant everything to Shahid, and even though he knew that she was going to die, her death came as a blow. Shahid attributed a lot of his own traits to Sufia and she was the most important woman in his life, one who had stood by him ever since he had decided to become a poet, at age nine, and around whom he had shaped his world. Shahid said that his mother's death was 'one of the most monstrous things' that had ever happened to him. In an interview in 2001, three years after her death, Shahid spoke about his mother and said: 'I still can't reconcile myself to the fact that she's gone; I just can't. It's been over three years.'[5] Though Shahid had been aware that her illness was terminal, that she was going to die sooner or later, there was a sense of disbelief in him. The rush of emotions and memories that followed her death turned the unfortunate situation even worse for Shahid. He didn't—or perhaps couldn't—write for a long time, because he was still coming to terms with a world without Sufia. When he eventually wrote, it was naturally about his mother and her death. In poems following Sufia's death, Shahid doesn't address grief but defines it. In 'Lenox Hill', all acts of injustice and all the sorrows of the world become a weighing scale with which he measures the grief caused by her death. Although he had written moving and poignant elegies, 'Lenox Hill' was unrivalled.

Looking at 'Lenox Hill', it is clear that his mother's death brought out in Shahid a side that discarded all reason, a side that he too was perhaps unaware of. He tried to push the boundaries of rationality to make sense of Sufia's death, but no matter what he scoured, it left him with no resolve. Memories from his childhood in Kashmir came gushing back, and he remembered the time when she dressed him as Krishna. In 'Lenox Hill', perhaps for the first time, Shahid allowed language to turn into an emotional vent. Whereas most poems lead the readers into different directions, here, the clarity exposes the poem itself, leaving no space for the readers to develop their own meaning. It points to only one word: 'mother'. In the envoi of the canzone, he truly explains the magnitude of loss he had experienced:

Do you hear what I once held back: in one elephant's
cry, by his mother's bones, the cries of those elephants

that stunned the abyss? Ivory blots out the elephants.
I enter this: *The Beloved leaves one behind to die.*
For compared to my grief for you, what are those of Kashmir,
and what (I close the ledger) are the griefs of the universe
when I remember you—beyond all accounting—O my mother?[26]

In free verse, with no limitations and no restraints, his emotions might have got the better of him. But the distance created by the formal structure disembodied the loss and turned it into a subject that he could write about. Each time 'Kashmir' or 'mother' is repeated—it is more than a lament, for it gives rise to a lasting cry. In an interview conducted after his mother's death, Shahid said: 'When you're dealing with painful subject matter . . . I would say definitely you need distancing devices. You can make that very choice to distance yourself from a subject matter, a thematic and aesthetic issue. But to actually serve that material you need a formal distancing device because otherwise you might end up sounding simply hysterical.'[7] Although 'Lenox Hill' is a wail that shatters glass and questions the universe for the poet's loss, it is only the door through which Shahid enters the space of mourning. The poems that follow use the historical Battle of Karbala as the backdrop.

It was Sufia's wish that she be buried in Kashmir. Iqbal remembers: 'Sometime before she died—I remember this very clearly—she had said to me: "*Ab hum udengey!*" There was a duality in the statement—she would fly off to the heavens but also fly back to Kashmir to be buried.'[8] Thus, after her death, the family started making arrangements for their travel back to Kashmir with her coffin. In an essay, Shahid wrote: 'My siblings, father, and I knew she would have wanted us to bring her back to Kashmir. So it was: Boston-Frankfurt-Delhi on a Lufthansa, and then the transfer to Indian Airlines for the trip from Delhi to Srinagar.'[9] Shahid also captured the journey in a twelve-part poem, 'From Amherst to Kashmir'. In the fourth part, 'Above the Cities', he traced the journey back to Kashmir on the Lufthansa flight:

> And any city
> I am leaving—even if one you've never
> seen—my parting words are for you alone. For
> where there is farewell,

you are there. And when there's a son, in any
language saying *Adieu* to his mother, she is
you and that son (*There by the gate*) is me, that
son is me. Always.[10]

'Only Karbala could frame our grief,' Shahid wrote in 'Memory',
the third section of the poem. He opened the poem with the Battle
of Karbala, about which his mother had narrated stories to him on
numerous occasions. He used it to evoke his mother and magnify
the loss in an operatic way, as only he could. 'From Amherst to
Kashmir' is heavily influenced by a Shia Muslim sense of loss.
Sufia often quoted from the Koran, offering metaphors and images
that Shahid interspersed throughout his poetry. In a couplet from
his ghazal 'In Arabic', he wrote: 'Ah! Bisexual Heaven: wide-
eyed houris and immortal youths! / To your each desire they say
Yes! O Yes! in Arabic'—an idea that was presented to him by his
mother, one summer in Kashmir. The Koran promises seventy-
two virgins, or houris, in heaven after one's death. However, Sufia
always questioned: 'What's there for me? What am I going to do
with virgins?'[11] Shahid used these moments in his poetry along
with the story of Karbala.

The Battle of Karbala and the martyrdom of Hussain are
among the most important moments in Shia history. Forty-
eight years after the death of Prophet Muhammad, his grandson,
Hussain, was killed in the Battle of Karbala by forces of Yazid I,
the second caliph of the Umayyad Caliphate. While on his way
to Kufa from Mecca, Yazid's forces stopped Hussain's caravan
at Karbala, cutting off the supply of water for days, leaving men,
women and children to die of thirst. The battle between Hussain
and Yazid was fought on the tenth Muharram, known as the Day
of Ashura. Hussain's caravan of less than a hundred people was
outnumbered by the Yazid forces. Soon, all of Hussain's men were
killed and only a few family members remained. Hussain pleaded

to the Yazid forces for water, only for his son. In response, they fired an arrow, killing the child in his arms. Hussain then stepped into the battle and fought the enemy. But eventually, he fell from his horse and was beheaded by Yazid's men.

It is this historical battle with which Shahid opens his poem 'From Amherst to Kashmir'. In the first section, 'Karbala: A History of "The House of Sorrows"', he elucidates the importance of the battle, and how, years before, at the site of Karbala, Jesus wept and said: 'At this site the grandson of Prophet Muhammad (Peace be upon him) will one day be killed.' Shahid had taken to reading the Koran seriously after the death of this mother. Hussain's martyrdom and the grief it caused across generations, struck a chord with him. Those lamentations were not very different from his own. In the poem, he equated his mother to Zainab, Hussain's sister who held the first *majlis* (lamentations) at Yazid's palace after being taken captive after the battle:

At my mother's funeral a mourner sang one of her favourite Kashmiri elegies, given to Zainab, in which her exile is nearly unbearable. Those words now are my mother's, for she too was tired, fighting death, from hospital to hospital, from city to city.[12]

Shahid merged the death of his mother with the Battle of Karbala, conveying the magnitude of the loss that he felt, but at the same time questioned: 'I who of passion / always make a holocaust, will there be a summer of peace?' In an unpublished essay, he wrote what it felt like to be in a world without his mother:

. . . [L]ast year, when I returned to Kashmir for my annual trip, I had found myself choked when the plane crossed the mountains into the Vale for I felt her absence, the fact that she won't be at the airport to welcome me home—her face suddenly glowing upon seeing me, as it glowed upon seeing any of her children.

And as I stepped out of the terminal, there was my father, looking lonely; we didn't have to say anything to converse that yes he knew I was missing her terribly and he missing terribly her presence by his side to welcome me.'[13]

Illustration 17: Shahid's apartment in Brooklyn, New York, 2001.

In the twelve parts of 'From Amherst to Kashmir', he traced their relationship and how, in the late '80s, when Shahid came to Srinagar, his mother helped him translate Faiz. In 'Summers of Translation', he remembered the moment and wondered why they didn't 'linger just a bit on Memory [Faiz's poem]', before he finally translated the poem and wrote, 'desolation's desert, I'm here with shadows / of your voice'. 'Bhajan Found on 78 RPM' is Shahid's translation of a bhajan that his mother would often sing. He extended his grief through a Ghalib ghazal, as translated grief. However, Shahid's rage finally came out as the poem 'From Amherst to Kashmir' ended, and all that he felt, emerged as a cry.

Not only did his mother's death change him, but in many ways it moved Shahid to the extent where he began to question the universe for an explanation of his mother's death. It was the pain and difference between the living and the dead that came to surface—how the living had to live in a world without the beloved, how the 'Beloved leaves one behind to die'. He understood mortality and had experienced the loss of people he had loved— from Begum Akhtar to James Merrill—but after his mother's death he began to sense a void. In the last section of the poem, he left the reader with a question, the same question that he perhaps asked the universe each day:

> *How dare the moon*—I want to cry out,
>   Mother—*shine so hauntingly out*
> *here when I've sentenced it to black waves*
> *inside me? Why has it not perished?*
>   *How dare it shine on an earth*
> *from which you have vanished?*[14]

During those days, Eqbal Ahmad would come over for dinner to Shahid's place almost every night. 'Eqbal broke down when he heard about my mother,' Agha Iqbal Ali remembers.[15] By that time, Shahid and Ahmad had known each other for some years and their friendship had solidified. Thus, when two years later, in 1999, Shahid was informed of Ahmad's death, it came as a blow for him. In her book *Boys Will Be Boys*, Sara Suleri Goodyear remembers how Shahid informed her of Ahmad's death over the telephone and how they both burst into tears.[16]

In those last four years, Shahid had lost three very important people in his life: James Merrill in 1995, his mother in 1997 and Eqbal Ahmad in 1999. What had seemed to him a very distant, perhaps unimaginable time, had dawned too soon. At this difficult time in his life, he had no other route to take but poetry, and thus when he wrote 'I Dream I Am at the Ghat of the Only World', he imagined himself in conversation with ghosts. He summoned Begum Akhtar as 'the night of ghazals come to an end', and opened the door of the house in Amherst only to see Eqbal. His mother was there and so were the words of James Merrill, who had left him a copy of his last collection in his will. He banged the doors of hell like Orpheus, looked for the departed and spoke to the oarsman who guided him to the other world, where those who he had lost were alive. He dreamt he was at the ghat of the world, after which nothing existed. These ghosts, who spoke to him and led him out of himself, comforted him with their words. Although this poem came to be considered his farewell to the world by many of his friends, at the time it consoled him and reminded him that 'Love doesn't help anyone finally survive'.[17]

SEVENTEEN

The Last Years

By the late '90s, Shahid had been awarded the Pushcart Prize for his poem 'A History of Paisley', a Guggenheim Foundation grant and an Ingram Merrill fellowship for his works. He had established his position as an eminent poet in both India and the United States. He was included in *The Best American Poetry* series, edited by John Hollander, alongside poets such as John Ashbery, Anthony Hecht, Charles Simic and Derek Walcott. By this time, he had become a famous poet who was known for his engaging readings and had read his poems at numerous universities, like Yale, Oberlin and Penn State, as well as at writers' workshops, like the Bread Loaf Writers' Conference, Academy of American Poets and Tucson Poetry Festival. *The Country without a Post Office* had started creating ripples in the Indian subcontinent, and a book of his poems was published as *Beloved Witness: Selected Poems* by Viking Penguin in 1992.

Not only had he established his place as an eminent poet but also as an excellent teacher. In the spring of 1999, Shahid was the visiting professor of creative writing at Princeton, and the same year, he left UMass and took a permanent teaching position at the University of Utah. In the spring of 2000, he was the visiting professor at New York University's graduate creative writing programme.

Around the same time Shahid moved to Manhattan, he came in contact with Izhar Patkin, an Israeli–American artist, and they became good friends. In 1981, Patkin had painted *Unveiling of a Modern Chastity*, the first painting about AIDS—painted even before the disease had a name—depicting wounds or sores erupting from a skin-like surface.[1] He soon started exhibiting at various galleries in New York City and gained a reputation for himself as one of the finest contemporary artists in America. When Anne MacDonald, a patron of art and literature whose circle included the likes of Kathy Acker and Dennis Cooper, asked Patkin if he wanted to be a part of her project—under which poems and art would be published together—he said yes. MacDonald, who was Patkin's friend and had exhibited his works, always felt that, as opposed to artists who managed to scrape by and make ends meet, writers lived up to the cliché and were always underpaid. She thus wanted to publish a series of books with writers and artists. Patkin suggested that a writer by the name of Edit DeAk do the writing. MacDonald flew her from New York to San Francisco and gave her an advance of thousands of dollars. But Edit ended up spending the money on smack, and the project came to a standstill. Soon, MacDonald started suggesting other poets and writers, but Patkin didn't seem interested.[2]

'Well, Anne, I'll do it,' Patkin told her each time. 'But I just don't feel it. There's no spark.'

MacDonald spent years searching for a writer for her project. Then, the American novelist Jim Lewis intervened and said to her: 'Well, Anne, you're doing it wrong. You're giving him American writers—they mean nothing to him. You need to find him somebody brilliant who is on the same wavelength. Someone from the Levant.'

'Who?' MacDonald asked.

'Well,' Lewis replied, 'how about Agha Shahid Ali?'[3]

Within a few weeks, Patkin received a FedEx box. MacDonald had bought all of Shahid's collections and sent them to him. Days later, Patkin called her and said: 'Bingo! This is perfect.' Shahid and Patkin first met in New York, and over the course of the next few months, they met numerous times, laughing and talking about everything under the sun. However, they refused to talk about the book. 'One year had passed,' Patkin remembers, 'but we never discussed the project. We were too busy talking about life and other things. We were more interested to know about each other.'[4]

Although he had never discussed it with Shahid, Patkin had already envisioned what he wanted to do with Shahid's poems. He wanted to make rooms full of veils out of his poems that one could enter. And he was taken aback when he found that Shahid had something similar in mind.

'Our meeting point should be the veil,' Shahid suggested.

'It's funny that a Jew and a Muslim should meet at the veil,' Patkin replied.

'So, then, how do you want to go about it?'

'Let's not do the Jew–Muslim, feel-good thing. Let's give them hate,' Patkin joked.

'Ah! Darling, perfect,' Shahid laughed. 'We should have separate book launches from the start, nobody should know we've been talking to each other. We're going to milk this to death!'

By the end of their meeting, they had decided a working title for the project: 'Veiled Threats'.

But sometime later, Patkin received a call from Shahid: 'Listen,' he said. 'We have to focus on the project. I've been diagnosed with brain cancer.'[5]

In December 1999, Shahid had a sudden blackout and fell in his bathroom, at his apartment near Washington Square Park in New York. He had just moved into the apartment after taking the position of visiting professor at NYU. Ashraf, who was with Shahid at his apartment, called an ambulance, and Shahid was rushed to the closest hospital—St Vincent's. Later, he was shifted to the NYU Langone medical centre. Just as in the case of his mother, the initial suspicion was that it was a tapeworm. The diagnosis came as a shock to everyone: a malignant tumour similar to that which had caused his mother's death.

Brain tumour, as far as medical research suggests, is not a hereditary illness. Shahid had once suggested, in an interview, his illness was a response to his grief: 'I don't want to dramatize,' he'd said, 'but sometimes I think that my own cancer started in response to the grief I had that my mother was gone.'⁶ Amitav Ghosh believes that the possibility of Shahid developing the same disease in such a short span of time was 'inexplicable'. The story Ghosh thinks of in relation to Shahid is that of the Mughal emperor Babur's death. Babur's son Humayun was extremely sick, and after all the remedies had failed, Babur sent the hakims away and announced that he himself was the only person who could save Humayun. 'Babur walked around his bed three times saying, "I bring it upon me, I bring it upon me, I bring it upon me." And from that moment, Humayun revived, and Babur was dead in a few months.'⁷

By spring 2000, Shahid had started chemotherapy at the NYU medical centre and was living in Manhattan. By August 2000, the family started looking for a place and eventually, Sameetah found an apartment in Brooklyn, close to Pratt, where she taught. It was a large apartment with a library on the second floor and a wraparound balcony. It was when Shahid moved to Brooklyn that he truly became friends with Amitav Ghosh, who lived a few blocks away from him. Both of them met regularly, either at Shahid's apartment or at Ghosh's, where they would be joined by other writers like Mohsin Hamid and Suketu Mehta. 'We would chat and hang out. One time Mohsin read the first part of *The Reluctant Fundamentalist*—it was like an *adda*,' Ghosh recalls. 'But Shahid and I spent much more time together. My children went to school there, and Shahid would often come with me when I went to pick them up.'

Shahid and Ghosh had known each other when they first met in Brooklyn. In 1998, Ghosh had quoted a line from 'The Country without a Post Office' in an article on Kashmir, and they had met on several occasions. 'Shahid was indescribable,' Ghosh remembers. 'The way he functioned, the way he slipped between languages. He was completely South Asian, but at the same time, he was completely at home with Americans. Shahid had a wider range of friends in America than anyone I knew. Everyone who saw him loved him.'

Although it seemed that Shahid was fine, the illness was getting to him, and it would manifest in different ways. Naturally, thoughts of death would resurface time and again, but Shahid kept his composure and tried to be as resolute as he could. Once, in December 2000, Kamila Shamsie had come over to his place for dinner, unaware that this was the last time she would meet him in person: 'At some point he made some reference to not knowing how long he'd be around. I said, "Shahid, are you getting morbid?" And he said, "Oh no. Not at all. It's just, whatever happens, I don't feel afraid."'[8]

In the spring of 2001, Shahid was the Sidney Harman Writer-in-Residence at Baruch College. This would be his last teaching appointment. By this time, Shahid's short-term memory as well as his vision had started getting affected. At his reading at Baruch College on 30 March 2001, the font size of poems had been magnified for him. For the entire summer after the course had ended, his sister Hena had come to stay with Shahid. His friends Forrest Gander and Daniel Hall visited him in Brooklyn very often. Gander remembers, 'If you asked him if he saw a plane in the sky, he'd glance up and say yes, although he was glancing in the wrong direction. He didn't want us to know how much of his faculties he was losing.'[9]

However, even during his illness, when his memory had started fading and he was, at times, confused, he tried to fight it as much as possible, and mostly, with humour. Whenever someone would call, the answering machine of his phone would announce: 'Whoever you are, pledge to me your undying love'. It would bring an instant smile on the face of whoever was calling.[10] But besides the humour, there was a sense of resignation in him, for he realized that his body was doing to him what it had done to his mother.

Illustration 18: Shahid reading at Baruch College, New York, where he was the Sidney Harman Writer-in-Residence, 30 March 2001.

Jason Schneiderman, who went to see him in Brooklyn, said that Shahid was in good spirits when he last met him. He said to Schneiderman that he was asking all his friends to pray for him. 'He was trying to get prayers from as many faith groups as possible to maximize the chance of his prayers being heard,' Schneiderman recalls. 'It was the same old Shahid. I knew that this was a charming and rehearsed speech (I do the same thing before I go to parties so I'll have something to say). But then he started it again. As he began to repeat the same words for the third time, I realized that he'd lost his short-term memory, and that he was slipping away.'[11]

By February 2001, Shahid was informed that he had less than a year left to live. This came as a setback for everyone around him. 'I remember how worry worked his brother Iqbal's face and tightened his gestures,' Gander wrote. 'I remember Iqbal measuring out pills, logging the medication times, scrupulously keeping the journal that we did not want to have started and that we did not want to end.'[12]

Soon after the final diagnosis in February 2001, Shahid called Patkin: 'I have a good news and a bad news. What would you like to hear first?' 'I said to Shahid let's get the bad news out of the way,' Patkin remembers, 'because he sounded so cheerful on the phone that day.' The bad news, Shahid informed him, was that he only had some more months left to live. Dazed, Patkin wondered what could possibly follow.

'The good news,' Shahid continued, 'is that I'm not abandoning our project. I'm going to finish the poem before I die.'

'Shahid,' Patkin replied, 'you don't have to worry about it. It doesn't matter.'

'Oh darling, are you crazy?' Shahid said to him on the phone. 'This is the *only* thing that matters.'[13]

Right after he was told that his time was limited, Shahid had a dream which led him to his final poem, one that, according to Daniel Hall, even the rationalists among them found disturbing.

'[When asked about the initial idea for a poem] there were two sorts of answers that he would give,' Amitav Ghosh remembers. 'One was: "I was playing with this line of Merrill's"—the usual poet-speak. Another response was, "It came to me in a dream", or "I had a vision". So much of his work came in this manner.'[14]

At times, Shahid's verses unfolded like a half-remembered dream, while on other occasions, they stemmed from actual dreams which he, like the Japanese film-maker Akira Kurosawa, magically transformed into narratives that spoke more of the reality. Even the word 'dream' recurs throughout his poetry, and from Shahid's journals, where he recorded his dreams, it is evident that he tried to take away as much as possible from his subconscious.

In the dream that he had right after his final diagnosis, Shahid lay on his bed as a faceless figure tried to attack him, and Shahid said to himself: 'Faceless, he could represent only two alternatives: / that he was either a conscious agent of harm, / or that he would unknowingly harm me anyway.' Those lines ended up as the epigraph to 'The Veiled Suite'.

Just a few weeks after their conversation, Patkin received a fax from Shahid. 'He'd sent the poem. It was a full-blown canzone.' Shahid couldn't write at the time, so he had dictated the canzone, a sixty-five line poem with a strict rhyme and metre—one of the toughest forms in poetry—to his friend Patricia O'Neill, who read aloud drafts of the stanzas to him and annotated lines so he could rework them later. Speaking about the canzone form, the poet Anthony Hecht once remarked, 'Having used the form he [Dante] could easily understand why no one had been tempted to write more than one.' 'The Veiled Suite' was Shahid's third canzone. So, correcting himself, Hecht later remarked that 'Shahid deserved to be in Guinness Book of Records for having written three canzones—more than any other poet.'[15]

'No mortal has or will ever lift my veil,'
he says. Strokes my arm. What poison is his eyes?
Make me now your veil then see if you can veil
yourself from me. Where is he not from? Which vale
of tears? Am I awake? There is little sense
of whether I am his – or he is my – veil.
For, after the night is fog, who'll unveil
whom? Either he knows he is one with the night
or is unaware he's an agent of night –
nothing else is possible (who is whose veil?)
when he, random assassin sent by the sea,
is putting, and with no sense of urgency,

the final touches on – whose last fantasy?[16]

'The Veiled Suite' was conceived at a time when Shahid was facing
the unknown. In it, he accumulated all that he had experienced
during those months when death began knocking on his door.
He transformed the veil not into an object that hides but into
that which reveals the persona and defines it. The ambiguous 'he'
whom Shahid addresses has been variously interpreted as an erotic
double, as death and, most importantly, as God. His subject, at
times, merges with him when he writes: 'There is little sense of
whether I am his—or he is my—veil'; and other times, he is 'an
agent of harm'. This dichotomy not only adds the complexity to
the poem but also defines the ambiguous relationship that 'he'
shares with Shahid.

In the poem, Shahid summons the Urdu tradition, where the
'he' could be read as a God, death or lover. Shahid himself is the
beloved. The question that Shahid asks in the poem is not 'where
is he from?', but 'where isn't he from?', further intoxicating the
relationship by turning the other into an omnipresent figure, one

who exists across all borders, from Vail, Colorado to the Ganges. 'I don't know whether I believe in God or not,' Shahid once said in an interview, 'but I do think I believe in many reasons for the belief in God. Even if you don't believe in God you may as well act as if God exists, because where do you turn in an hour of uncertainty? Then you turn to the realm that goes beyond the rational or undercuts the rational. And that's when religion does help, can help. Or ritual elements of religion. So in pure rational terms, whether I believe in God I don't think I can answer. As such I might say no. But I still think, it's a good idea to believe in God.'[17]

When Shahid wrote, 'No mortal has or ever will lift my veil', or 'When I meet his gaze, there is again the veil', he evoked the Sufi idea of distance from the other which manifests itself as the veil. According to Ghosh, Shahid's poetic drive came from 'something completely different', which was what made him an authentic figure. Shahid's contemporaries viewed him in a different light, not as a modern poet. Many, including Ghosh, believe that it is impossible to understand Shahid within the rules and confines of modern rationality; that his work, spirit and his understanding of the world really came from a different place; that fundamentally, Shahid was a mystic comparable only to Sufi saints of Kashmir.

What makes 'The Veiled Suite' a truly marvellous poem is not its content or subject matter but the language and the approach. The more one reads the poem, the more it withdraws and the more it reveals. It challenges the commonsensical understanding of the world—of life, of death, of God—and by doing so, challenges reality. It is the final poem in the famous American critic Harold Bloom's *Till I End My Song: A Gathering of Last Poems*. In this anthology, Bloom collected the last poems of a hundred poets over the previous four centuries, starting from Edmund Spenser and ending with Shahid. In the book, Bloom wrote about 'The Veiled Suite':

The title poem is his last and perhaps his strongest, a shapely canzone founded upon a personal dream of dying that is also an encounter with an erotic double. I can hear the influence of James Merrill but assimilated to Ali's own rich cultural heritage. It is one of the most haunting of all last poems.[18]

Illustration 19: Shahid in Brooklyn, New York, 2001.

By the spring of 2001, Shahid's chemotherapy had stopped and the doctors had started giving him radiation therapy, because of which his head had to be shaved. When he saw the solemn faces of his friends and family, he would say: 'Cheer up! I look like Yul Brynner. The Americans find me sexy.'[19] In a moment, he transmuted a morbid situation into a lively and memorable moment. At the hospital, Shahid was confronted with gloomy faces each time. Gander remembers 'the look on their suddenly upraised faces when one morning Shahid was called and he stood, with our help, and shuffled down the hallway singing, "That's the way, uh huh, uh huh, I like it, uh huh, uh huh."'[20] During another visit to the hospital, Shahid asked the orderly where he was from. When the response was Ecuador, Shahid suddenly came to life and said: 'Spanish . . . I've always wanted to learn Spanish. Just to read Lorca.' The orderly was surprised and quoted a few lines in Spanish, which Shahid then repeated as they made their way to the car: '*La Cinque de la Tarde, la Cinque de la Tarde* . . .'[21]

But Shahid's condition was deteriorating, and everyone around him was concerned. In July 2001, Hena and Izhar sent Shahid's reports to Memorial Sloan Kettering Cancer Center. Shahid went there accompanied by Hena, Iqbal and Patkin. One of the interviews at Sloan was conducted by a south Indian doctor. In order to check to what extent the cancer had affected Shahid, the doctor asked him to spell 'world'. Upon hearing that, Shahid replied, 'I beg your pardon. What are you saying?' Shahid couldn't understand the word he had just uttered. But neither could Iqbal, who was sitting right next to Shahid: 'He was saying it in a funny way—even I couldn't understand it.' Frustrated, the doctor said: '*Duniya! Duniya! Duniya!*' 'Oh! you mean 'world'?' Shahid laughed, and then spelt it out.[22]

Once the doctors had analysed the reports and conducted the interviews, they placed Shahid into the drug trials. Upon hearing that, he turned to Iqbal and asked: 'What do you think?' Iqbal, at the time, was a little apprehensive and asked the doctors some more questions, like what was the phase of the trials, if they would give high dosage since they had mentioned that the family had kept him in good physical condition, and if he would be ported (a port that is used to deliver chemotherapy). However, after hearing all the answers, Iqbal wasn't convinced about the treatment since it was still in an initial testing stage. He said no to Shahid, and they walked away.

But the decision had been bothering Iqbal. When Iqbal expressed this concern to Shahid's neurologist Dr Steven V. Pacia, he arranged a meeting with Oliver Sacks, the famous neurologist who had written numerous books about the mind and its workings. In August 2001, Iqbal and Shahid went to see Sacks at his home. Sacks wanted to run a few tests and conduct interviews. In one such interview after the initial meeting, Sacks took a $5 bill out of his pocket and asked Shahid who was on it. Shahid didn't remember the name but said, 'The one who freed all the slaves.'

By this time, even his long-term memory had been impacted.[23] Some days, he would ask where his mother was, if she was still alive. On hearing the answer, he would break into tears, as if he had heard the news of her death for the first time. But he tried to keep his memory alive, and one way of doing that was music. He would often sing the songs of Begum Akhtar, humming them in a muffled voice in his room. When he was alone, he would play his favourite tracks, like 'I Shall be Released' by The Band, and sing along. Although singing these songs helped him to some extent, it was poetry that really rekindled his spirit and memory.

Even when his long-term memory was faltering, Shahid's poetic side had remained unaffected. His craft was the only thing that he lived by, and thus he channelled all his energy towards poetry. He started to train his memory by rote learning the poems he loved. He forced himself to memorize John Milton's 'Lycidas', Matthew Arnold's 'Dover Beach' and a number of Shakespeare's sonnets—forwards and backwards. At the NYU medical centre, Shahid was often given a plastic contraption in which he had to blow—it was an exercise to test his lungs and strength. As he did that, even though he could no longer write, the poems were still magically coming to him. While blowing and inhaling the air, Shahid put together his final couplet:

> Drink this rain-dark rum of air
> column of breath column of air.[24]

Illustration 21: *The Veil Suite* (detail), Izhar Patkin, 2007.

Illustration 22: *The Veil Suite* (detail), Izhar Patkin, 2007.

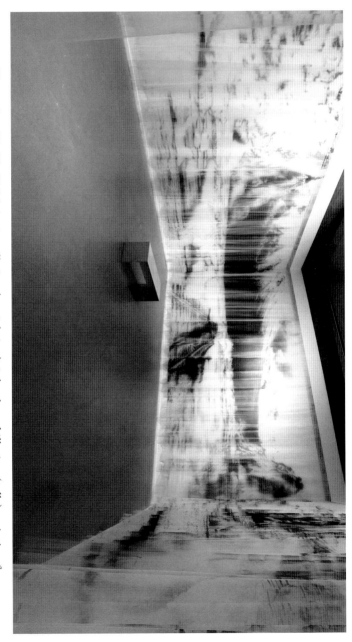

Illustration 23: *The Veil Suite*, installation (partial view), ink, pleated illusion (tulle), painting for four walls, 14 x 22 x 28 feet (426.72 x 670.56 x 762 cm), Izhar Patkin, 2007.

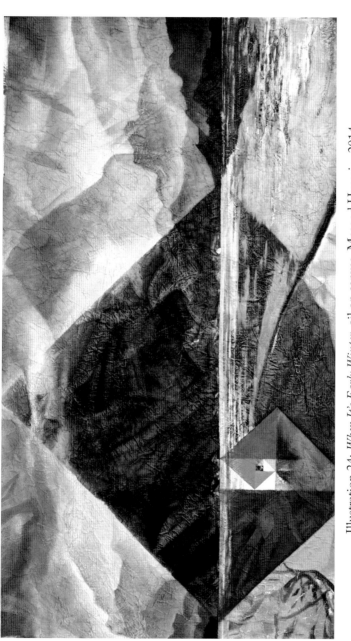

Illustration 24: *When It's Early Winter*, oil on canvas, Masood Hussain, 2014.

Illustration 25: *Autumn Refrain in Kashmir*, oil on canvas, Masood Hussain, 2014.

This was one of the things that caught Sacks's attention. Sacks had never seen anything like it before. Here was a man whose memory was failing, but he could still memorize and recite poetry. After meeting both Shahid and Iqbal separately, he called them together and asked Iqbal what he wanted to do. Iqbal said that he would like to take Shahid to his home, in Amherst; and Sacks said that would be ideal. Although the decision was made, Iqbal asked Sacks if he could write a report. In the report, Sacks wrote that Shahid only had some weeks, or at the most months, left to live, which aligned with what Shahid's doctor had said in February 2001. Shahid moved from Brooklyn to Amherst. Iqbal had bought a house in Amherst that had a bedroom on the ground floor with wheelchair access from the driveway. Sacks also sent the report to the Northampton area. Soon, Shahid was placed under hospice care.

When a nurse at the hospice read Shahid's name, she said that she wanted to go take care of him. Shahid had been in contact with her during his mother's illness and she had come once, a few days before Sufia's death. Over the next three months, from August to the end of November, Shahid didn't spend a single day alone. His siblings and his father were there, and people were flying in from all parts of America to see him. Each day, someone would come to Amherst to see him, and Iqbal, along with others, would cook for the guests. The setting was incomparable. A fellow poet, a friend, a teacher was dying, and there was incredible grief, but at the same time, there was joy. There was music each night, the ghazals of Begum Akhtar and all the songs that he loved, filled the air. There was always a festive atmosphere. What was beautiful about it was that Shahid wanted this atmosphere of joy: 'I love it that so many people are here. I love it that people come and there's always food. I love this spirit of festivity; it means that I don't have time to be depressed,' Shahid once said.

But by that time Shahid had become aware of his mortality as well. Naturally, he was afraid. 'I get scared of the unknown,' he said. 'I don't know what's going to happen. I really have to face the fact that I can't read. Because these letters don't stay still, they just dance along the page, which is so frustrating. I'm very scared.'[25] Even during those days, when he was suffering from short-term memory loss, with the knowledge that death was imminent, Shahid made sure that he tried his best to remain true to himself. When someone informed Kamila Shamsie that Shahid was about to die and was suffering from memory loss, she called him and was 'afraid he wouldn't know who I was'. Shamsie recalls that Shahid, on the phone, said 'Darling' in his expansive way and responded as he always had. He then made some joke about wanting to come see the Queen of England and asked Shamsie: 'But is she ready for me?'[26]

Shahid was dying with the knowledge that he would be missed, that along with his poetic legacy, he was leaving behind a lasting legacy of love and friendship. Hena came for months, and would cook and care for Shahid, while Sameetah and Iqbal were always by his side. For almost a year, his friends regularly came to see him for extended weekends, as well as other people, like his students and fellow poets and writers. 'It exhausted Shahid, but he wanted the company more than anything else,' Gander recalls. 'At the end, he was in Massachusetts with a hospice-care person by his bed who seemed to me possessive of him. When I sat down, he began to squeeze Shahid's medicinal pump. Shahid very much wanted to speak. He was trying to talk to me, but the hospice person kept pumping him with morphine—for the perceived discomfort. Even at this stage, at the end, in his illness, in his drugged state, he fought hard to keep his dignity.'[27]

It was while he was in Amherst with Iqbal that Shahid received the news that *Rooms Are Never Finished* had been shortlisted as a finalist for the 2001 National Book Award. Because Shahid couldn't go for the official recitation, he sent the only person he trusted with his poetry, Iqbal. Shahid asked Iqbal to recite 'Lenox

Hill' to him, and while Iqbal was reciting the poem, Shahid asked him to read the poem as it was, without making it sound poetic. When Iqbal started reciting again, Shahid stopped him once more and said: 'It's elephants, not elephant.' It turned out that there were two errors in the book. Two of Shahid's friends had corrected the proofs and had failed to rectify the mistake along with the date of Sufia's death. Even at that stage, when he referred to 9/11 as 'the thing that happened in New York', when nothing made sense to him, Shahid was able to identify a flaw in his poem's rhyme scheme and catch the error. But his condition was slowly getting worse. During the final days, he was put on an automated delivery of morphine, although he tried to stay cheerful as best he could.

Hena came to see Shahid on Thanksgiving, 22 November 2001, after which she went back to Kirksville. When she called some days later, the nurse told her that Shahid only had a little time left and that she should come and meet him for the last time. Soon, Hena was back in Amherst. On 6 December 2001, Iqbal called Patricia O'Neill and told her that Shahid was in his last hours. She drove to Amherst, where, upon meeting Shahid, she realized that he was already losing consciousness. When she reached, his eyes were closed. She took his hand and hummed a line from his favourite song, 'That's the way, ah hah, I like it', to which Shahid smiled. That was their last exchange. By 7 December, everyone knew that these were his final moments, and his family had said their goodbyes. The nurse, Patricia Bruno from VNA Hospice Care, saw him at 10 p.m. When she went in again at 2.30 a.m. to check on him, Shahid had already drawn his last breath, the one taken but never given back.

Epilogue

After You

In 'The Last Saffron', Shahid had made a prophecy: 'I will die, in autumn, in Kashmir, / and the shadowed routine of each vein, / will almost be news.'[1] Even though Shahid had expressed his desire to go back to Kashmir to die numerous times, he later changed his mind and chose Northampton as his final resting place, which wasn't too far from Dickinson's grave in West Cemetery in Amherst—an idea that made him happy. State laws prevented his family from interring him within twenty-four hours of death, which is the Muslim custom, and thus on 10 December 2001, which, coincidentally, was Dickinson's birth anniversary, Shahid was buried at the Bridge Street Cemetery in Northampton.

'There was an ice storm the night before his funeral, and in the morning the sunlight glittered off the icicles hanging from the trees in the cemetery, where his family and friends gathered,' Christopher Merrill recalled in his book. 'The bearded imam recruited to perform the burial service kept losing his place—a public display of incompetence that would have sent Shahid into paroxysms of laughter. Adjacent to his grave was the headstone of a veteran from World War II. "Shahid's dream has finally come true: to lie next to a man in uniform!" someone quipped, bringing

171

a note of levity to a somber occasion.'² The tombstone on his
grave read 'Agha Shahid Ali / Kashmiri-American Poet', and the
epitaph was a couplet from 'In Arabic': 'They ask me to tell them
what Shahid means: Listen, Listen: / It means "the beloved" in
Persian, "witness" in Arabic.'

Illustration 20: Shahid's grave at Bridge Street Cemetery,
Northampton, Massachusetts.

A day after his death on 8 December, newspapers around the
world mourned the death of the poet. An obituary appeared in
the *New York Times* with the heading 'Agha Shahid Ali, 52, a
Poet Who Had Roots in Kashmir', while the *Boston Globe* ran as
obituary an article they had written for his National Book Award
nomination. In India, *Greater Kashmir*'s Sunday supplement,
Sensor, was dedicated to Shahid and included essays by his friends
and admirers, as did *Tehelka*. Other tributes and obituaries
appeared in the *Washington Post, Rattapallax, Jacket Magazine*, the
Annual of Urdu Studies and *Catamaran* magazine, which dedicated

its first issue to Shahid. 'His poems will keep him alive, maybe,' Rukun Advani wrote in *Tehelka* on 9 December 2001, 'but only among those who never knew him and therefore missed out on seeing and hearing what being preternaturally alive means as an everyday, ordinary practice.'[3] Kamila Shamsie echoed the same sentiments in her essay 'Agha Shahid Ali, Teacher':

> After his funeral, a friend of mine—another former student of Shahid's (it occurred to me that only after he died could I start calling myself a 'former student' of his) wrote to say: 'It didn't seem possible or moral or legal, that we were all there to acknowledge the death of that most alive of men.'[4]

Six months before his death, Marty Williams had suggested to Christopher Merrill that they make a ghazal chain for Shahid. The ghazal, to which, by the end, more than a hundred poets had contributed couplets, was published in *Rattapallax*. In her essay 'The Chain', Grace Schulman—who was asked by Williams to deliver the ghazal chain to Shahid and obtain the signature couplet, the makhta—wrote about the ghazal: 'Contributors were of many poetic persuasions. Now and always, poets have been known to be feisty protectors of their ideologies. Not so here. The ghazal chain is a dance of diverse performers. In it, remarkably, such things as poetic divisions, loyalties, and doctrines fade in the greater effort to honor Shahid.'[5]

Shahid knew that he would survive in the memories of those who knew him, but he wanted to live, not just through people but also the written word. He had made it extremely clear months before his death when he said to Ghosh: 'You must write about me.'[6] In the poems written by his friends, students and colleagues, Shahid emerges as a guiding light whose voice lingers on in the words of those who loved and admired him.

* * *

The University of Massachusetts Amherst, where Shahid had spent almost six years, from 1993 to 1997, as the director of the Master of Fine Arts programme, held a memorial tribute for Shahid in May 2002, while the graduate creative writing programme at New York University paid tribute to Shahid by announcing the Agha Shahid Ali Memorial Readings, which, over a span of four editions—held in 2002, 2003, 2006 and 2009—hosted poets such as Meena Alexander, Forrest Gander, Galway Kinnell, Michael Palmer, Elise Paschen, Tom Sleigh, Michael Collier, Marilyn Hacker and Carolyn Forché, among others.

In 2003, the University of Utah, where Shahid was supposed to return after serving as a visiting professor at New York University in spring 2000, established an annual poetry prize called the Agha Shahid Ali Poetry Prize, 'honouring the memory of a celebrated poet and a beloved teacher'.[7] The prize has been awarded to seventeen poets ever since. The same year, *Call Me Ishmael Tonight: A Book of Ghazals* was posthumously published, by W.W. Norton & Company. The collection, put together by Shahid's siblings, Iqbal and Hena, celebrates Shahid's legacy as a pioneer of ghazals in the English language. Although his name had already become synonymous with the form, it was the first time Shahid's ghazals were compiled in one collection.

In 2009, Patricia O'Neill, Shahid's colleague at Hamilton College, received permission from the college's Digital Humanities Initiative to set up a repository of Shahid's materials. With Shahid's sister Hena as the co-director, she established an archive of Shahid's papers, letters and other documents that he had left with Iqbal to preserve his legacy. 'The pilot project was really a proof of concept for the idea of digital archives and what they could do to make a writer's process available to an international community, something which seemed especially important in Shahid's case,' O'Neill noted.[8]

By 2012, the college received Shahid's entire collection to create the Agha Shahid Ali Special Collections. 'Mostly I remember being overwhelmed by the amount of material,' she recalled, 'hundreds of books, at least ten large plastic containers of papers, videos, audio tapes, at least three file cabinets full of papers, piles of telephone bills, mortgages, doctors' bills, student papers in boxes—and none of it organized at all.'[9] The archives have been safeguarding Shahid's legacy ever since his death and have invited numerous researchers and writers to study the life of one of the most celebrated South Asian poets. Without their support and help, the research for this biography would have been an inconceivable task.

* * *

Some months before his death, Shahid had handed a canzone to the Israeli–American artist Izhar Patkin. 'The Veiled Suite', Shahid's final poem, was written especially for Patkin as part of the collaboration between them. In 2009, the poem was published for the first time in its entirety in *The Veiled Suite: The Collected Poems*. The cover of the collection carried a painting by Patkin— his visual rendition of the poem.

It took Patkin six more years after Shahid's death to finish the project in 2007. 'For me, it took years to understand his poem,' Patkin recollected in an interview. 'And I could only understand the rhythm after I color-coordinated all the rhymes in order to understand the structure of the canzone. It's this endless euphoria with that work, endless inspiration. I hope that it'll be for other people as well, it must.'[10] Patkin turned Shahid's poem into a room which one could enter, filled with tulle curtains on which he'd painted. 'For me, the curtain is a canvas. The metaphor: painting is a veil,' he said in an interview.[11] According to the poet Ariana Reines, 'Patkin's curtain rooms are narratives with no beginning and no end—circles one can enter anywhere, in the same way that one can enter a poem one knows well at any point and still accede to the whole of it . . . Patkin's curtained rooms (or curtain rooms) play on the word stanza, which, while referring to poetry, also—in Italian—means "room".'[12]

Since he died in 2001, many of Shahid's poems have been rendered visually by artists across the world, one of them being the Kashmiri artist Masood Hussain. In the summer of 2000, Masood Hussain met Shahid at his house in Rajbagh, which wasn't far from the college where Hussain taught. Shahid was sitting in the veranda, typing on his electronic typewriter. 'Here are some couplets that I have written keeping you in mind. I want you to paint them,' Shahid had said to him. 'I thought to myself: These are about Kashmir's beauty and changing of seasons—why is he giving them to me?' Hussain remembered.[13] He took them and left, not knowing then that it was the last time they would meet.

In his paintings, he interpreted Shahid's couplets, which he saw everywhere. He saw the 'crimsoned spillages' when during a curfew he saw from his window a worker on the street crying in pain—a stray bullet had hit him. In Gurez Valley in Kashmir, as he watched the pyramid-shaped Habba Khatoon peak, named after the famous Kashmiri poet (legend has it that the sixteenth-century poet disappeared in this mountain, looking for her lover Yusuf Shah Chak, the emperor of Kashmir, who was imprisoned by Akbar), he was reminded of another couplet that Shahid had handed him:

Such tinted distances that you can touch the shades that have disappeared till summer!

The coming cold testifies to the earth's fidelities, stronger here than anywhere else . . .[14]

'Maybe if he was here, he would be happy,' Hussain said, years later, recollecting the process of painting Shahid's couplets, staring at the canvasses. 'I wish he were. I read his poems often. I look for hope. I wish I could untie these knots in my lifetime.'[15]

Another artist who was inspired by Shahid's poems was Nilima Sheikh. Her collection *Each Night Put Kashmir in Your Dreams*—which borrows its title from a line from Shahid's poem 'I See Kashmir from New Delhi at Midnight'—focuses on the 'magical history and contentious present of Kashmir'.[16] Many of the titles of the paintings from the series—'Farewell' and 'Son et Lumiere'—come from Shahid's poems, and she draws numerous motifs, ideas and stories from *The Country without a Post Office*.

* * *

On 5 August 2019, Jammu and Kashmir's special status was revoked by the Indian government. Three days into the curfew, when the news finally reached Kashmir, almost 10,000 people protested after the Friday prayers; the mainstream Indian media announced that there was peace in the Valley.[17] Over the next few months, all landlines, cellphone and Internet services were shut down in the Valley, curfew-like restrictions were imposed prohibiting all public movement, and the post offices were shuttered by the Indian Postal Services—Kashmir had once again turned into 'The Country without a Post Office'.[18] Id-uz-Zuha, the Muslim festival of sacrifice, fell on 11 August, but there was no possibility of celebration; it was impossible to utter 'Id *mubarak*' on the telephones to loved ones. As Kashmir was cut off from the whole world, Shahid was summoned to speak for those who were silenced. His poems flooded the Internet. And why not? This passage from 'The Blessèd Word', written more than two decades ago, could be describing the terrible events of 2019—how Id-uz-Zuha was observed under curfew, how thousands of sons were detained by the armed forces,[19] and God's inability to help the people:

> It was Id-uz-Zuha: a record of God's inability, for even He must melt sometimes, to let Ishmael be executed by the hands of his father. Srinagar was under curfew. The identity pass may or may not have helped in the crackdown. Son after son—never to return from the night of torture—was taken away.[20]

Today, readers of poetry throughout the world turn to *The Country without a Post Office* to understand Kashmir, perhaps because poetry can teach us what history misses out on. 'I learnt of Agha Shahid Ali, predictably, from a Kashmiri friend returning from London, on a wet and foggy evening in JNU,' Manash Firaq, a poet and writer based in Delhi, remembers. 'Poets introduce you to the invisible corners of a place, where memory is stored. Shahid wove Kashmir—its poetic myths, its precarious and fragile relationship with history—into my imagination. Suddenly, a Nerudaesque spirit would leap out of a poem: "Freedom's terrible thirst, flooding Kashmir, / is bringing love to its tormented glass."'

The Country without a Post Office is remembered each time the word 'Kashmir' is mentioned, at least in the literary realm. Salman Rushdie used a part of Shahid's poem 'Farewell' as the epigraph to his novel *Shalimar the Clown*, which is set in Kashmir. *A Desolation Called Peace: Voices from Kashmir*, an anthology of essays about Kashmir, edited by Ather Zia and Javaid Iqbal Bhat, as well as Basharat Peer's poignant memoir *Curfewed Night*—both draw their titles from Shahid's poems. But while Shahid's work has become a window to Kashmir for people around the globe, for the Kashmiris his poetry is a mirror.

'For many of us, growing up amid this horror,' the novelist Mirza Waheed recalls, 'it was Shahid who shone a light on the darkness. I remember I had a near visceral reaction when I first read

Country . . . It was akin to listening to someone making sense of my world to me for the first time.'[21] Ather Zia, a poet and associate professor of anthropology at the University of Colorado Boulder, believes that, 'In need of an urgent voice to express their pain and suffering, Shahid's poetry became a tongue for many young and old Kashmiris, that his powerful poetry about his suffering homeland, bolstered by his long visits, which were followed by his untimely death in 2001 sealed his status as the balladeer of Kashmir's political tragedy.'[22] For Zia, as for many Kashmiri poets and writers, Shahid remains a formal spirit who has not only provided her with a direction but also hope. 'Shahid has remained a constant companion in my psychic universe and often appears in my verses, sometimes guiding and sometimes questioning,' she said to me in an interview. 'One of his famous poems, "Stationery" in *The Half-Inch Himalayas*, ends with a simple hope: "The world is full of paper. Write to me." This became a personal invocation, ensuring poetry stayed a constant companion as I began the journey of anthropology.'[23]

Today, Shahid's collection has gained iconic status and is perhaps the only poetry collection that has been discussed and quoted from in the Indian parliament, not once but twice.[24] In 2016—three years after the collection was released as a separate volume in India by Penguin Random House—a controversy ensued after a reading of *The Country without a Post Office* at Jawaharlal Nehru University in New Delhi. A poster of the cultural evening, titled 'Poetry Reading – The Country without a Post Office', stated that the event was against the 'judicial killing of Afzal Guru and Maqbool Bhat' and in 'solidarity with the struggle of the Kashmiri people for their democratic right to self-determination'.[25] The matter was debated on all media channels and soon became a topic of national interest. It was discussed in Parliament by the then Union urban development minister, M. Venkaiah Naidu, who took the title of Shahid's collection a little too literally and asked: 'The heading of the poster says: "A Country without a Post Office." Is India without post office? The entire world is looking towards India under the great leadership of Shri Narendra Modiji today.'[26]

What began with mere ignorance slowly snowballed into an unintentional burlesque, and more absurdity followed. A man from Hyderabad, blissfully unaware of Shahid's collection, filed a Right to Information application asking how many post offices there were in Jammu and Kashmir.[27] I can imagine Shahid laughing hysterically at this farce, as he so often did at similar misinterpretations. *The Country without a Post Office* has undoubtedly established its place as one of the most important texts of South Asian literature and continues to keep Shahid's memory alive. Although it is one of his most important collections and deserves all the attention it attracts, Shahid's legacy is as diverse and complex as his personality. The timelessness of the subject matter and aesthetic beauty of his poems have allowed him to not only stay relevant but have also added to his enduring legacy as one of the most beloved poets around the globe.

* * *

'One of the few things I don't lie about is poetry,' Shahid once said. 'Everything else, I lie about.'[28] From the age of nine to the final days of his life, Shahid remained true and devoted to his art, spending an enormous amount of time to embroider himself into the fabric of his poetry. Today, two decades after his death, Shahid's spirit lives on in his works, which have a life of their own. As for his poems, they have turned into a spacious and boundless room, an archive of longings, dotted, like a museum, with pieces from his life, open to all.

Acknowledgements

This biography would not have been possible without help from Agha Shahid Ali's family. I wish to thank Shahid's brother Agha Iqbal Ali for his invaluable insights, his unwavering belief in this project and his assistance over the last four years. Without him, I would have been lost. I would also like to express my gratitude to Shahid's sisters, Hena Ahmad and Sameetah Agha, who candidly spoke about their brother, for their encouragement, guidance as well as their hospitality at their home in Srinagar.

For sharing the memories of their beloved friend, teacher and colleague and for their generosity, I would like to thank Patricia O'Neill, Saleem Kidwai, Vidur Wazir, Suvir Kaul, Aman Nath, Anuradha Dingwaney Needham, Lawrence Needham, Padmini Mongia, Rukun Advani, Christopher Merrill, Irfan Hasan, Masood Hussain, Daniel Hall, Forrest Gander, Kamila Shamsie, Jason Schneiderman, Anthony Lacavaro, Izhar Patkin and Amitav Ghosh. The fact that everyone contributed so open-heartedly and helped a first-time biographer in his attempt to write about their friend speaks volumes.

At the Beloved Witness Project, a Mellon-funded digital archive of video-taped readings, personal documents, letters and manuscripts of Agha Shahid Ali at Hamilton College, I would like to thank Christian Goodwill, Mark Tilson and Dr Robert Paquette. Without their cooperation and help, it would have been an impossible task to finish this book. Additionally, for the permission to use materials from the archives, I thank the Agha Shahid Ali Literary Trust.

For permission to use their paintings and photographs, I wish to thank Izhar Patkin, Masood Hussain, Neil Davenport and Saleem Kidwai.

At Sangam House Writers' Residency, where most of this book was written in November 2019, Arshia Sattar, D.W. Gibson, Giles Hazelgrove, Pascal Sieger and Trupti Prasad for allowing me a chance to be a part of a wonderful experience.

For taking out the time to read the manuscript and for their suggestions and critique, I am deeply grateful to Ranjit Hoskote and Jeet Thayil. I would also like to gratefully acknowledge the help from Sadia Khatri, Akhil Katyal, Kazim Ali and various other researchers and writers whose works helped me discover various aspects of Shahid's poetry and life.

At Writers' Side literary agency, Kanishka Gupta, who believed in this project when it was nothing but a two-page summary. At Penguin Random House, I would like to thank Elizabeth Kuruvilla, Vineet Gill and Antra K for bringing the manuscript to life, and Swati Chopra and Milee Ashwarya for commissioning this book.

For their friendship and counsel: Manash Firaq Bhattacharjee, Richa Burman, Karan Chauhan, Varnika Kundu, Ankita Sharma and Mayank Kundu. I also wish to thank Satvika Kundu for reading the manuscript several times and for all the insights and edits that have improved my writing over the last five years. Lastly, I would like to thank my family. Pranshu Kapoor, for constantly being there every time a decision had to be made, and my parents, Shruti and Daman Kapoor, for their constant support and for introducing me to poetry at a young age, without which I would never have discovered Shahid.

Notes

Introduction

1. T.S. Eliot, 'The Waste Land', *The Waste Land and Other Poems* (London: Faber and Faber, 1999).
2. Lawrence Needham, 'Interview with Agha Shahid Ali', *The Verse Book of Interviews: 27 Poets on Language, Craft & Culture*, ed. Brian Henry and Andrew Zawacki (Seattle: Wave Books, 2005).
3. Christian Benvenuto, 'Interview with Agha Shahid Ali', *Massachusetts Review*, vol. 43, no. 2 (Summer, 2002), p. 262.
4. Agha Shahid Ali, 'The Walled City: Seven Poems on Delhi', *In Memory of Begum Akhtar* (Calcutta: Writers Workshop, Kolkata, 1979).
5. Agha Shahid Ali, 'Dismantling Some Silences', *Poetry East*, no. 27, Spring 1989.
6. Benvenuto, 'Interview with Agha Shahid Ali', p. 262.
7. T.S. Eliot, 'Tradition and Individual Talent', *Selected Essays, 1917–1932*, (Boston: Houghton Mifflin Harcourt, 1942).
8. Amitav Ghosh, 'Ghat of the Only World: Agha Shahid Ali in Brooklyn', *Nation*, 4 January 2002.
9. Rukun Advani, 'Agha Shahid Ali: A Few Memories', *Tehelka*, 9 December 2001.

Prologue

1. William Dalrymple, 'The Bloody Legacy of the Indian Partition', *New Yorker*, 22 June 2015.
2. Aparna Basu, 'Back Cover', *Mridula Sarabhai: Rebel With a Cause* (Oxford: Oxford University Press, 1996).
3. Agha Iqbal Ali, personal interview, Srinagar, May 2018.
4. Agha Shahid Ali, 'Lenox Hill', *The Veiled Suite: The Collected Poems* (New Delhi: Penguin Random House, 2010), p. 247.

Chapter 1: The Season of Plains

1. Agha Shahid Ali, 'A Darkly Defense of Dead White Males', *Poet's Work, Poet's Play: Essays on the Practice and Art*, ed. Daniel Tobin and Pimone Triplett (Ann Arbor: University of Michigan Press, 2008), p. 147.
2. Ibid.
3. Agha Shahid Ali, 'The Season of Plains', *The Veiled Suite*.
4. Amitav Ghosh, 'Ghat of the Only World: Agha Shahid Ali in Brooklyn', *Nation*, 4 January 2002.
5. Agha Shahid Ali, 'The Season of Plains', *The Veiled Suite*.

Chapter 2: Jamia

1. Agha Ashraf Ali, 'My Life Has Been Wedded to Excellence', interview by Majid Maqbool, *Greater Kashmir*, 14 March 2015.
2. Mohammad Ashraf Khaja, 'A European Account of the Socio–Economic and Educational Condition of Kashmiris under the Dogra Rule: A Critical Appraisal', *International Journal of Scientific and Research Publications*, vol. 6, issue 11, November 2016.
3. M.Y. Ganai, 'Modern Education and the Rise of Political Consciousness in Kashmir (1846–1931)', *Proceedings of the Indian History Congress*, vol. 65, 2004, pp. 891–900.
4. Fayaz Ahmad Kotay, 'Educational Backwardness of Muslims in Princely Kashmir: An Inferential Analysis of the Legacy of Dogra

Raj', *Asian Journal of Research in Social Sciences and Humanities*, vol. 5, no. 1, January 2015, pp. 106–119.

5. Agha Ashraf Ali, 'My Life Has Been Wedded to Excellence'.
6. Ibid.
7. Ibid.
8. Ibid.
9. Ashish Kochhar, 'Jamia Millia Islamia: An Ode to Unity', Live History India.
10. 'I would like to see the Punjab, North-West Frontier Province, Sind and Baluchistan amalgamated into a single State. Self-government within the British Empire, or without the British Empire, the formation of a consolidated North-West Indian Muslim State appears to me to be the final destiny of the Muslims, at least of North-West India.' See Muhammad Iqbal's '1930 Presidential Address' to the 25th Session of the All-India Muslim League, Allahabad, 29 December 1930, http://www.columbia.edu/itc/mealac/pritchett/00islamlinks/txt_iqbal_1930.html
11. Agha Shahid Ali, 'The Walled City: Seven Poems on Delhi', *In Memory of Begum Akhtar* (Calcutta: Writers Workshop, 1979).
12. Agha Ashraf Ali, 'My Life Has Been Wedded to Excellence'.
13. Agha Iqbal Ali, personal interview, Srinagar, May 2018.

Chapter 3: Harmony 3

1. Agha Iqbal Ali, personal interview, Srinagar, May 2018.
2. Agha Ashraf Ali, 'My Life Has Been Wedded to Excellence'.
3. Vidur Wazir, personal interview, Srinagar, September 2018.
4. Christian Benvenuto, 'Interview with Agha Shahid Ali', *Massachusetts Review*, vol. 43, no. 2 (Summer, 2002), p. 262.
5. Agha Shahid Ali, 'Introduction', *The Rebel's Silhouette: Selected Poems* (Amherst: University of Massachusetts Press, 1995).
6. Sameetah Agha, personal interview, Srinagar, July 2019.
7. Vidur Wazir, personal interview, Srinagar, September 2018.
8. Agha Iqbal Ali, personal interview, Srinagar, May 2018.
9. Agha Shahid Ali, 'A Darkly Defense of Dead White Males', *Poet's Work, Poet's Play: Essays on the Practice and Art*, ed. Daniel Tobin

and Pimone Triplett (Ann Arbor: University of Michigan Press, 2008).

10. Ibid.
11. Vidur Wazir, personal interview, Srinagar, September 2018.
12. Agha Iqbal Ali, personal interview, Srinagar, May 2018.
13. Ibid.
14. Agha Ashraf Ali, personal interview, Srinagar, September 2018.
15. Jackie Lyden, 'Interview with Agha Shahid Ali', NPR, 28 July 2001.
16. Ibid.
17. Agha Iqbal Ali, personal interview, Srinagar, May 2018.

Chapter 4: The Awakening

1. Christopher Merrill, '"A Route of Evanescence": Agha Shahid Ali in America', *Mad Heart Be Brave: Essays on the Poetry of Agha Shahid Ali* (Ann Arbor: University of Michigan Press, 2017), p. 90.
2. Jackie Lyden, 'Interview with Agha Shahid Ali', NPR, 28 July 2001.
3. Sufia Agha, letter to Agha Shahid Ali, 25 January 1979, Special Collections at Hamilton College, Burke Library, Hamilton College, Clinton, New York.
4. Agha Ashraf Ali, 'My Life Has Been Wedded to Excellence'.
5. Agha Shahid Ali, 'Application to Ball State', Special Collections at Hamilton College, Burke Library, Hamilton College, Clinton, New York.
6. Agha Iqbal Ali, personal interview, Srinagar, May 2018.
7. Bruce King, 'Agha Shahid Ali's Tricultural Nostalgia', *Journal of South Asian Literature*, vol. 29, no. 2, 1994, pp. 1–20.
8. Amitav Ghosh, 'Ghat of the Only World: Agha Shahid Ali in Brooklyn'.
9. Agha Shahid Ali, 'Snowmen', *The Veiled Suite*.
10. Eric Gamalinda, 'Poems Are Never Finished: A Final Interview with Agha Shahid Ali', *Poets & Writers*, March–April, 2002.
11. Ibid.
12. Agha Shahid Ali, 'Note Autobiographical–2', *In Memory of Begum Akhtar* (Calcutta: Writers Workshop, Kolkata, 1979).

13. Agha Shahid Ali, 'Prayer Rug', *The Veiled Suite*.
14. Vidur Wazir, personal interview, Srinagar, September 2018.
15. Kamla Kapur, 'Dancing with Agha Shahid Ali', ThePrint.com, 4 June 2019.
16. Agha Shahid Ali, 'Introducing', *In Memory of Begum Akhtar*.
17. Saleem Kidwai, personal interview, Lucknow, March 2018.
18. Akhil Katyal, 'I Swear I Have My Hopes: Agha Shahid Ali in Delhi', Kafila, 30 January 2011.
19. T.S. Eliot, 'Tradition and the Individual Talent', *Selected Essays*, 1917–1932 (Boston: Houghton Mifflin Harcourt, 1942).
20. Agha Shahid Ali, 'A Darkly Defense of Dead White Males', *Poet's Work, Poet's Play: Essays on the Practice and Art*, ed. Daniel Tobin and Pimone Triplett (Ann Arbor: University of Michigan Press, 2008).
21. Ibid.
22. Agha Shahid Ali, 'The Love Song of J. Alfred Prufrock', box 9, 156.1, Special Collections at Hamilton College, Burke Library, Hamilton College, Clinton, New York.
23. Ibid.
24. Agha Ashraf Ali, personal interview, Srinagar, September 2018.
25. Agha Iqbal Ali, personal interview, Srinagar, May 2018.
26. Ibid.

Chapter 5: In Streets Calligraphed with Blood

1. Rehan Ansari, 'Agha Shahid Ali: Calligraphy of Coils', *Himal Southasian*, 1 March 1998.
2. Akhil Katyal, 'I Swear I Have My Hopes: Agha Shahid Ali in Delhi', Kafila, 30 January 2011.
3. Saleem Kidwai, in an interview with the author, Lucknow, March 2018.
4. Akhil Katyal, 'I Swear I Have my Hopes: Agha Shahid Ali in Delhi'.
5. Ibid.
6. Saleem Kidwai, in an interview with the author.
7. Ibid.
8. Ibid.

9. Sejal Shah, 'The World Is Full of Paper. Write to Me', Asian American Writers' Workshop, 8 December 2013.

10. Agha Shahid Ali, 'Flight from Houston in January', *The Veiled Suite*.

11. Saleem Kidwai, in an interview with the author.

12. Octavio Paz, *In Light of India* (New Delhi: Rupa Publications, 1990).

13. Ibid.

14. Agha Shahid Ali, 'The Walled City: Seven Poems on Delhi'.

15. Octavio Paz. 'The Tomb of Amir Khusro', *The Poems of Octavio Paz* (New York: New Directions Publishing, 2012).

16. Agha Shahid Ali, 'The Walled City: Seven Poems on Delhi'.

17. Ibid.

18. Agha Shahid Ali, 'After Seeing Kozintsev's *King Lear* in Delhi', *The Veiled Suite*.

19. Agha Shahid Ali, 'A Darkly Defense of Dead White Males'.

20. Ibid.

21. Ibid.

22. Agha Shahid Ali, 'Indian Poetry in English', box 3, folder 1, Special Collections at Hamilton College, Burke Library, Hamilton College, Clinton, New York.

Chapter 6: Akhtari

1. Saleem Kidwai, personal interview, Lucknow, March 2018.

2. Ibid.

3. Ibid.

4. Rita Ganguly, *Ae Mohabbat, Reminiscing Begum Akhtar* (Delhi: Stellar Publishers, 2008).

5. Priya Ramani, 'What a Life', Livemint, 7 November 2008.

6. Rita Ganguly, *Ae Mohabbat, Reminiscing Begum Akhtar*.

7. Regula Burckhardt Qureshi, 'In Search of Begum Akhtar: Patriarchy, Poetry, and Twentieth-Century Indian Music', *The World of Music*, vol. 43, no. 1, 2001, pp. 97–137.

8. Agha Iqbal Ali, personal interview, Srinagar, May 2018.

9. Ibid.

10. Ibid.

11. Debojit Dutta, 'Watch Begum Akhtar Sing as Kaifi Azmi Recites 2 Exquisite Ghazals', Antiserious, 30 June 2016.
12. Regula Burckhardt Qureshi, 'In Search of Begum Akhtar: Patriarchy, Poetry, and Twentieth-Century Indian Music'.
13. Amitav Ghosh, 'Ghat of the Only World: Agha Shahid Ali in Brooklyn'.
14. Agha Shahid Ali, 'Introduction', *The Rebel's Silhouette: Selected Poems* (Amherst: University of Massachusetts Press, 1995).
15. 'Agha Shahid Ali on Faiz Ahmad Faiz' (audio), Poets House, 19 November 1998.
16. Amitav Ghosh, 'Ghat of the Only World: Agha Shahid Ali in Brooklyn'.
17. Priya Majithia, 'Celebrating the Queen of Ghazals', *Ahmedabad Mirror*, 23 October 2014.
18. Saleem Kidwai, personal interview, Lucknow, March 2018.
19. Agha Shahid Ali, 'In Memory of Begum Akhtar', *The Veiled Suite*.
20. Naomi Lazard, 'Introduction', *The True Subject: The Poetry of Faiz Ahmad Faiz* (Princeton: Princeton University Press, 1988).
21. Rehan Ansari, 'Agha Shahid Ali: Calligraphy of Coils', *Himal Southasian*, 1 March 1998.
22. Agha Shahid Ali, 'Snow on the Desert', *The Veiled Suite*.
23. Agha Shahid Ali, 'On Teaching English', *Illustrated Weekly of India*, May 1976.
24. 'Agha Shahid Ali, A Poet of Loss', *First City*, February 1991.
25. Ibid.
26. Agha Shahid Ali, 'Leaving Your City', *The Veiled Suite*.

Chapter 7: A Year of Brilliant Water

1. Eric Gamalinda, 'Poems Are Never Finished: A Final Interview with Agha Shahid Ali', *Poets & Writers*, March–April, 2002.
2. Amitav Ghosh, 'Ghat of the Only World: Agha Shahid Ali in Brooklyn'.
3. Ibid.
4. Sejal Shah, 'The World Is Full of Paper: Write to Me', Asian American Writers' Workshop, 8 December 2013.

5. Agha Shahid Ali, 'Today, Talk is Cheap. Call Somebody', *The Veiled Suite*.
6. Agha Shahid Ali, 'Agha Shahid Ali: The Lost Interview', interview by Stacey Chase, *The Café Review*, Spring 2011.
7. Christopher Merrill, *Self-Portrait with Dogwood* (San Antonio: Trinity University Press, 2017).
8. Agha Iqbal Ali, personal interview, Srinagar, May 2018.
9. Anuradha Needham, personal interview, New Delhi, January 2020.
10. Padmini Mongia, personal interview, New Delhi, June 2019.
11. Eric Gamalinda, 'Poems Are Never Finished: A Final Interview with Agha Shahid Ali'.
12. Agha Shahid Ali, 'Agha Shahid Ali: The Lost Interview'.
13. Eric Gamalinda, 'Poems Are Never Finished: A Final Interview with Agha Shahid Ali'.
14. T.S. Eliot, 'Tradition and the Individual Talent'.
15. Eric Gamalinda, 'Poems Are Never Finished: A Final Interview with Agha Shahid Ali'.
16. Ibid.
17. Elain Showalter, *A Jury of Her Peers: American Women Writers from Anne Bradstreet to Annie Proulx* (London: Little, Brown Book Group, 2009).
18. Undated interview, box 9, section 2, Special Collections at Hamilton College, Burke Library, Hamilton College, Clinton, New York.
19. Ibid.

Chapter 8: In Exodus, I Love You More

1. Agha Shahid Ali, letter to Suzanna Tammien at Wesleyan University Press, 15 February 1994, Special Collections at Hamilton College, Burke Library, Hamilton College, Clinton, New York.
2. Salman Rushdie, letter to Agha Shahid Ali, 29 March 1988, Special Collections at Hamilton College, Burke Library, Hamilton College, Clinton, New York.
3. Khademul Islam, 'Our Story of Dhaka Muslin', *AramcoWorld*, May–June 2016.
4. Agha Shahid Ali, 'The Dacca Gauzes', *The Veiled Suite*.

5. Padmini Mongia, personal interview, New Delhi, June 2019.
6. Anuradha Dingwaney, personal interview, New Delhi, January 2020.
7. Christopher Merrill, *Self-Portrait with Dogwood* (San Antonio: Trinity University Press, 2017).
8. Christian Benvenuto, 'Interview with Agha Shahid Ali', *Massachusetts Review*, vol. 43, no. 2, Summer 2002, p. 262.
9. Agha Shahid Ali, 'A Darkly Defense of Dead White Males'.
10. Ibid.
11. Ibid.
12. Ibid.
13. Christian Benvenuto, 'Interview with Agha Shahid Ali'.
14. Agha Shahid Ali, 'Agha Shahid Ali: The Lost Interview', Interview by Stacey Chase, *The Café Review*, Spring 2011.
15. Agha Shahid Ali, 'Postcard from Kashmir', *The Veiled Suite*.
16. Undated interview, box 9, section 2, Special Collections at Hamilton College, Burke Library, Hamilton College, Clinton, New York.

Chapter 9: A Memory of Musk

1. Agha Shahid Ali, 'The True Subject: The Poetry of Faiz Ahmed Faiz', *Grand Street*, vol. 9, no. 2, 1990, pp. 129–138.
2. Ibid.
3. Edward Said, 'The Mind of Winter: Reflections on Life in Exile', *Harper's Magazine*, September 1984.
4. Agha Shahid Ali, 'The True Subject: The Poetry of Faiz Ahmed Faiz'.
5. Agha Shahid Ali, '*The Rebel's Silhouette*: Translating Faiz Ahmad Faiz', *Between Languages and Cultures: Translation and Cross-Cultural Texts*, ed. Anuradha Dingwaney and Carol Maier (Pittsburgh: University of Pittsburgh Press, 1996).
6. Faiz Ahmad Faiz, letter to Agha Shahid Ali, 6 October 1980, Special Collections at Hamilton College, Burke Library, Hamilton College, Clinton, New York.
7. Hena Ahmad, personal interview, Srinagar, July 2019.
8. Naomi Lazard, 'Translating Faiz', *Columbia*, June 1958.

9. Agha Shahid Ali, 'Letter to Naomi Lazard', Special Collections at Hamilton College, Burke Library, Hamilton College, Clinton, New York.

10. Agha Shahid Ali, 'From Urdu to English', letter to the editor, *Columbia*, October 1985.

11. Agha Shahid Ali, 'The True Subject: The Poetry of Faiz Ahmed Faiz'.

12. Agha Shahid Ali, 'Introduction', *The Rebel's Silhouette: Selected Poems*.

13. Ibid.

14. Naomi Lazard, 'Translating Faiz'.

15. Agha Shahid Ali, 'Introduction', *The Rebel's Silhouette: Selected Poems*.

16. Agha Shahid Ali, 'Homage to Faiz Ahmad Faiz', *The Veiled Suite*.

17. Agha Shahid Ali, 'Interview with Agha Shahid Ali', by Lawrence Needham, *The Verse Book of Interviews: 27 Poets on Language, Craft & Culture*, ed. Brian Henry and Andrew Zawacki (Seattle: Wave Books, 2005).

18. Nick Owchar, 'A Tribute to Troubadours' Language of Love', *Los Angeles Times*, 27 June 2002.

19. 'The Go Betweens: Leah Goldberg, Yehuda Amichai, and the Figure of the Poet-Translator', *A Companion to Translation Studies*, ed. Catherine Porter and Sandra Bermann (New York: Wiley, January 2014).

Chapter 10: A Route of Evanescence

1. 'New Mexico: Taos and Alcalde', Tate, https://www.tate.org.uk/whats-on/tate-modern/exhibition/georgia-okeeffe/room-guide/room-seven

2. Agha Shahid Ali, 'Agha Shahid Ali: The Lost Interview', interview by Stacey Chase, *The Café Review*, Spring 2011.

3. Agha Shahid Ali, 'A Darkly Defense of Dead White Males'.

4. Rehan Ansari, 'Agha Shahid Ali: Calligraphy of Coils', *Himal Southasian*, 1 March 1998.

5. Christopher Merrill, Skype interview, July 2019.

6. Agha Shahid Ali, 'I Dream I Return to Tucson in the Monsoons', *Massachusetts Review*, vol. 29, no. 4, 1988.

7. Agha Shahid Ali, letter to Agha Ashraf Ali, Special Collections at Hamilton College, Burke Library, Hamilton College, Clinton, New York.

8. Ibid.

9. Ibid.

10. James Merrill, 'Back Cover', Agha Shahid Ali, *A Nostalgist's Map of America* (New York: W.W. Norton & Company, 1991).

11. Agha Shahid Ali, 'The Keeper of the Dead Hotel' at Ball State University, 1997, Special Collections at Hamilton College, Burke Library, Hamilton College, Clinton, New York.

12. Agha Shahid Ali, 'A Nostalgist's Map of America', *The Veiled Suite*.

13. Rehan Ansari, 'Agha Shahid Ali: Calligraphy of Coils', *Himal Southasian*, 1 March 1998.

14. Agha Shahid Ali, 'A Nostalgist's Map of America'.

15. Emily Dickinson, 'Letter to Elizabeth Holland', 1866, *The Letters of Emily Dickinson* (Cambridge: Belknap Press of Harvard University Press, 1986).

16. Undated interview, box 9, section 2, Special Collections at Hamilton College, Burke Library, Hamilton College, Clinton, New York.

17. Agha Shahid Ali, Rafael Campo, Gertrude Clarke Whittall Poetry and Literature Fund, and Archive of Recorded Poetry and Literature, 'Agha Shahid Ali and Rafael Campo reading their poems in the Mumford Room, Library of Congress', audio, 1 February 1999.

18. Ibid.

19. Agha Shahid Ali, 'When on Route 80 in Ohio', *The Veiled Suite*.

Chapter 11: Shahid, the Teacher

1. Patricia O'Neill, email interview, June 2019.

2. Ibid.

3. Kamila Shamsie, 'Agha Shahid Ali, Teacher', *Annual of Urdu Studies*, vol. 17, 2002.

4. Rukun Advani, 'Agha Shahid Ali: A Few Memories', *Tehelka*, 9 December 2001.
5. Agha Shahid Ali, 'My Teaching Philosophy', Special Collections at Hamilton College, Burke Library, Hamilton College, Clinton, New York.
6. Ibid.
7. Christopher Merrill, Skype interview, July 2019.
8. Sejal Shah, 'The World Is Full of Paper. Write to Me', Asian American Writers' Workshop, 8 December 2013.
9. Ibid.
10. Kamila Shamsie, email interview, October 2019.
11. Jason Schneiderman, email interview, October 2019.
12. Ibid.
13. Kamila Shamsie, email interview, October 2019.

Chapter 12: My Dearest James

1. Christopher Merrill, Skype interview, July 2019.
2. Agha Shahid Ali, 'Shahid on Merrill', box 9, section 1, Special Collections at Hamilton College, Burke Library, Hamilton College, Clinton, New York.
3. Aman Nath, personal interview, New Delhi, June 2019.
4. Patricia O'Neill, email interview, June 2019.
5. Agha Shahid Ali, 'Shahid on Merrill'.
6. Ibid.
7. 'James Merrill at Amherst', *Amherst*, Summer 2015, https://www.amherst.edu/amherst-story/magazine/issues/2015-summer/james-merrill-at-amherst/node/612710
8. Langdon Hammer, *James Merrill: Life and Art* (New York: Knopf Doubleday Publishing Group, 2015).
9. Agha Shahid Ali, 'Shahid on Merrill'.
10. Interview with Sameetah Agha, Srinagar, 2019.
11. Agha Shahid Ali, 'Letter to James Merrill', 30 September 1990, Special Collections at Hamilton College, Burke Library, Hamilton College, Clinton, New York.

12. Christian Benvenuto, 'Interview with Agha Shahid Ali', *Massachusetts Review*, vol. 43, no. 2, Summer 2002, p. 262.

13. Agha Shahid Ali, 'Shahid on Merrill'.

14. Agha Shahid Ali, 'I Dream I Am at the Ghat of the Only World', *The Veiled Suite*.

15. Ibid.

16. Agha Shahid Ali, 'Introduction', *Ravishing DisUnities: Real Ghazals in English* (Middletown: Wesleyan University Press, 2000).

17. Agha Shahid Ali, 'Shahid on Merrill'.

Chapter 13: The Cry of the Gazelle

1. Agha Shahid Ali, 'The Ghazal in America: May I?', *After New Formalism: Poets on Form, Narrative, and Tradition*, ed. Annie Finch (Ashland: Story Line Press, 1999), p. 123.

2. Ibid.

3. Aijaz Ahmad (ed.), 'Introduction', *Ghazals of Ghalib* (New York: Columbia University Press, 1971), pp. vii–xxviii.

4. Agha Shahid Ali, 'Introduction', *Ravishing DisUnities: Real Ghazals in English* (Middletown: Wesleyan University Press, 2000).

5. Aijaz Ahmad (ed.), 'Introduction', *Ghazals of Ghalib*.

6. Phyllis Webb, 'Preface', *Water and Light: Ghazals and Anti-Ghazals* (Toronto: Coach House Press, 1984).

7. Ibid.

8. Agha Shahid Ali, 'Introduction', *Ravishing DisUnities: Real Ghazals in English*.

9. Ibid.

10. Ibid.

11. Ibid.

12. Ibid.

13. Agha Shahid Ali, 'The Ghazal in America: May I?'.

14. Agha Shahid Ali, 'Tonight', *The Veiled Suite*.

15. Agha Shahid Ali, 'Introduction', *Ravishing DisUnities: Real Ghazals in English*.

16. In *The Veiled Suite*, the ghazal was removed from the section which included ghazals from *Call Me Ishmael Tonight* because of

the repetition. However, in *Call Me Ishmael Tonight*, both versions ('Arabic' and 'In Arabic') were included by Agha Iqbal Ali to show the metamorphoses of Shahid's ghazals over time.

17. Agha Iqbal Ali, personal interview, Srinagar, May 2018.
18. Agha Shahid Ali, 'A Darkly Defense of Dead White Males', *Poet's Work, Poet's Play: Essays on the Practice and Art*, ed. Daniel Tobin and Pimone Triplett (Ann Arbor: University of Michigan Press, 2008).
19. Agha Shahid Ali, 'In Arabic', *The Veiled Suite*.
20. Christopher Merrill, *Self-Portrait with Dogwood* (San Antonio: Trinity University Press, 2017).
21. Christian Benvenuto, 'Interview with Agha Shahid Ali', *Massachusetts Review*, vol. 43, no. 2, Summer 2002, p. 262.
22. Ibid.
23. Ibid.

Chapter 14: Kashmir, Kaschmir, Cashmere

1. Edward W. Said, Aga Shahid Ali, Ibrahim Abu-Lughod, Akeel Bilgrami, Eqbal Ahmad, 'The Satanic Verses', *New York Review of Books*, 16 March 1989.
2. Akhil Katyal, 'I Swear I Have my Hopes: Agha Shahid Ali in Delhi', Kafila, 30 January 2011.
3. David Barisman, *Confronting Empire: Interviews with Eqbal Ahmad* (London: Pluto Press, 2000.)
4. Ibid.
5. Agha Iqbal Ali, personal interview, Srinagar, May 2018.
6. 'Agha Shahid Ali at Eqbal Ahmad's Farewell Dinner, Hampshire College, 1997' (video), Archive.org.
7. Ibid.
8. Victoria Gatenby, 'Kashmiris Mark 28th Anniversary of Gaw Kadal Massacre', Al Jazeera, 21 January 2018.
9. Mirza Waheed, 'Recollections of a Long Siege in Kashmir', *Time*, 19 November 2019.
10. Mridu Rai, *Hindu Rulers, Muslim Subjects: Islam, Rights, and the History of Kashmir* (London: Hurst, 2004), p. 27.

11. Ibid.
12. Rahul Tripathi, 'Instrument of Accession: From 1947 Till Date', *Economic Times*, 6 August 2019.
13. Prabash K. Dutta, 'Kashmir: How Line of Control Has Changed in 70 Years', *India Today*, 9 August 2019.
14. A.G. Noorani, 'Roots of the Kashmir Dispute', *Frontline*, 27 May 2016.
15. Manavi Kapur, 'A Timeline of Key Events That Shaped the Unique Identity of Kashmir within India', Quartz India, 6 August 2019.
16. Sumantra Bose, 'The Evolution of Kashmiri Resistance', Al Jazeera, 2 August 2011.
17. Parveena Ahangar, 'My Son Is One of Kashmir's "Disappeared". When Will India Tell the Truth about Their Fate?', *Guardian*, 12 September 2019.
18. 'Thousands of Unmarked Graves Discovered in Kashmir', Amnesty USA, 23 August 2011.
19. Rebecca Ratcliffe, 'India Set to Withdraw Kashmir's Special Status and Split It in Two', *Guardian*, 5 August 2019. (Although according to official figures released by the government, the death toll is much lower, at 41,000 between 1990 and 2017—roughly four deaths a day. See, Jayanth Jacob and Aurangzeb Naqshbandi, '41,000 Deaths in 27 Years: The Anatomy of Kashmir Militancy in Numbers', *Hindustan Times*, 25 September 2017.)
20. Agha Shahid Ali, 'The Obscenity of Normalcy', box 9, section 1, Special Collections at Hamilton College, Burke Library, Hamilton College, Clinton, New York.

Chapter 15: Crimsoned Spillages

1. Agha Shahid Ali, 'The Blessed Word: A Prologue', *The Veiled Suite*.
2. Agha Shahid Ali, 'The Obscenity of Normalcy', box 9, section 1, Special Collections at Hamilton College, Burke Library, Hamilton College, Clinton, New York.
3. Eric Gamalinda, 'Poems are Never Finished: A Final Interview with Agha Shahid Ali', *Poets & Writers*, March–April, 2002.

4. Amitav Ghosh, 'Ghat of the Only World: Agha Shahid Ali in Brooklyn'.

5. Agha Shahid Ali, 'Interview with Agha Shahid Ali', by Lawrence Needham, *The Verse Book of Interviews: 27 Poets on Language, Craft & Culture*, ed. Brian Henry and Andrew Zawacki (Seattle: Wave Books, 2005).

6. Agha Shahid Ali, 'A Darkly Defense of Dead White Males'.

7. Irfan Hasan, personal interview, Srinagar, September 2019.

8. Agha Shahid Ali, 'The Obscenity of Normalcy', box 9, section 1, Special Collections at Hamilton College, Burke Library, Hamilton College, Clinton, New York.

9. Agha Shahid Ali, 'Shahid on Merrill', box 9, section 1, Special Collections at Hamilton College, Burke Library, Hamilton College, Clinton, New York.

10. Agha Shahid Ali, 'The Correspondent', *The Veiled Suite*.

11. Joseph Heller, 'Joseph Heller, The Art of Fiction No. 51', interview by George Plimpton, *Paris Review*, issue 60, Winter 1974.

12. Agha Shahid Ali, 'After an August Wedding in Lahore', *The Veiled Suite*.

13. Aliza Noor, 'How, 30 Years Ago, Kashmiri Pandits Became Refugees in Their Country', TheQuint.com, 19 January 2020.

14. Mridu Rai, 'Kashmir: The Pandit Question', interview by Azad Essa, Al Jazeera, 1 August 2011.

15. Aliza Noor, 'How, 30 Years Ago, Kashmiri Pandits Became Refugees in Their Country'.

16. Ibid.

17. Mridu Rai, in the interview with Al Jazeera, notes that there is an ambiguity in terms of the number of Pandits who left the Valley in 1989, primarily because 'the numbers of Pandits in the valley in 1989 can only be adduced from the census of 1941', which 'listed a little fewer than 79,000 Pandits in the valley'. She says: 'Using the rough measure of the average decennial growth rate in the state as a whole, available through the censuses up to 1941 and then the 2001 census, the number of Kashmiri Pandits living in the valley before 1990 that they arrive at is about 160,000 to 170,000.'

18. Mridu Rai, 'Kashmir: The Pandit Question'.

19. Agha Shahid Ali, 'I See Kashmir from New Delhi at Midnight', *The Veiled Suite*.

20. Heather Marring, 'Conversation with Agha Shahid Ali', *Center: A Journal of the Literary Arts*, February 2002, pp. 57–69.

21. Joseph Brodsky, 'A Guide to a Renamed City', *Less Than One: Selected Essays* (New York: Farrar, Straus & Giroux, 1986).

22. Deborah Myers-Weinstein, 'A Case Study in Assimilation and Identity: Osip Mandelstam', *European Judaism: A Journal for the New Europe*, vol. 30, no. 1, 1997, pp. 34–50.

23. Masood Hussain, 'Since Last We Met: Painting Agha Shahid Ali's Couplets on Kashmir', TheWire.com, 7 December 2016.

Chapter 16: From Amherst to Kashmir

1. T.S. Eliot, 'The Waste Land', *The Waste Land and Other Poems* (London: Faber and Faber, 1999).

2. Amitav Ghosh, 'Ghat of the Only World: Agha Shahid Ali in Brooklyn'.

3. Amitav Ghosh, personal interview, Goa, January 2020.

4. Agha Shahid Ali, 'Lenox Hill', *Rooms Are Never Finished* (New York: W.W. Norton & Company, 2001).

5. Eric Gamalinda, 'Poems Are Never Finished: A Final Interview with Agha Shahid Ali'.

6. Agha Shahid Ali, 'Lenox Hill', *The Veiled Suite*.

7. Christian Benvenuto, 'Interview with Agha Shahid Ali'.

8. Agha Iqbal Ali, personal interview, Srinagar, May 2018.

9. Agha Shahid Ali, 'The Obscenity of Normalcy', box 9, section 1, Special Collections at Hamilton College, Burke Library, Hamilton College, Clinton, New York.

10. Agha Shahid Ali, 'Above the Cities', *Rooms Are Never Finished* (New York: W.W. Norton & Company, 2001).

11. Agha Iqbal Ali, personal interview, Srinagar, May 2018.

12. Agha Shahid Ali, 'Karbala: A History of "The House of Sorrows"', *The Veiled Suite*.

13. Agha Shahid Ali, 'The Obscenity of Normalcy', box 9, section 1, Special Collections at Hamilton College, Burke Library, Hamilton College, Clinton, New York.

14. Agha Shahid Ali, 'By the Waters of the Sindh', *The Veiled Suite*.

15. Agha Iqbal Ali, personal interview, Srinagar, May 2019.

16. Sara Suleri Goodyear, *Boys Will Be Boys* (Chicago: University of Chicago Press, 2003).

17. Agha Shahid Ali, 'I Dream I Am at the Ghat of the Only World', *The Veiled Suite*.

Chapter 17: The Last Years

1. Sarah Douglas, 'Is This the First AIDS Artwork?', *ARTnews*, 18 September 2015.

2. Izhar Patkin, 'Anne Macdonald (1942–2018)', *ArtForum*, 26 October 2018.

3. Izhar Patkin, Skype interview, August 2019.

4. Ibid.

5. Ibid.

6. Eric Gamalinda, 'Poems Are Never Finished: A Final Interview with Agha Shahid Ali'.

7. Amitav Ghosh, personal interview, Goa, January 2020.

8. Kamila Shamsie, email interview, October 2019.

9. Forrest Gander, email interview, June 2019.

10. Forrest Gander, 'One Death', *A Faithful Existence: Reading Memory and Transcendence* (Berkeley: Counterpoint, September, 2005).

11. Jason Schneiderman, email interview, October 2019.

12. Forrest Gander, 'One Death'.

13. Izhar Patkin, Skype interview, August 2019.

14. Amitav Ghosh, personal interview, Goa, January 2020.

15. Anthony Hecht, 'Letter to Agha Shahid Ali', Special Collections at Hamilton College, Burke Library, Hamilton College, Clinton, New York.

16. Agha Shahid Ali, 'The Veiled Suite', *The Veiled Suite: Collected Poems* (New York: W.W. Norton & Company, 2009).

17. Heather Marring, 'Conversation with Agha Shahid Ali', *Center: A Journal of the Literary Arts*.

18. Harold Bloom, *Till I End My Song: A Gathering of Last Poems* (New York: Harper, 2010).

19. Irfan Hasan, personal interview, Srinagar, September 2019.
20. Forrest Gander, 'One Death'.
21. Amitav Ghosh, 'Ghat of the Only World: Agha Shahid Ali in Brooklyn'.
22. Agha Iqbal Ali, personal interview, Srinagar, May 2018.
23. Ibid.
24. Agha Shahid Ali, 'Air', *The Veiled Suite*.
25. Heather Marring, 'Conversation with Agha Shahid Ali'.
26. Kamila Shamsie, email interview, October 2019.
27. Forrest Gander, email interview, June 2019.

Epilogue

1. Agha Shahid Ali, 'The Last Saffron', *The Veiled Suite: The Collected Poems*.
2. Christopher Merrill, *Self-Portrait with Dogwood* (San Antonio: Trinity University Press, 2017).
3. Rukun Advani, 'Agha Shahid Ali: A Few Memories', *Tehelka*, 9 December 2001.
4. Kamila Shamsie, 'Agha Shahid Ali, Teacher', *Annual of Urdu Studies*, vol. 17, 2002.
5. Grace Schulman, 'The Chain', *Mad Heart Be Brave: Essays on the Poetry of Agha Shahid Ali* (Ann Arbor: University of Michigan Press, 2017).
6. Amitav Ghosh, 'The Ghat of the Only World: Agha Shahid Ali in Brooklyn'.
7. Agha Shahid Ali Poetry Prize website, https://uofupress.lib.utah.edu/agha-shahid-ali-poetry-prize/
8. Maureen Nolan, 'Beloved Witness, Beloved Friend', *Hamilton*, Spring–Summer 2017.
9. Ibid.
10. 'A Conversation with Izhar Patkin and Ariana Reines', May 2009, izharpatkin.com/ veiled_threats/conversation_reines_text.html
11. Ibid.
12. Ibid.
13. Masood Hussain, personal interview, Srinagar, September 2018.

14. Ibid.
15. Ibid.
16. 'Nilima Sheikh: Each Night Put Kashmir in Your Dreams', Art Institute Chicago, https://www.artic.edu/exhibitions/1880/nilima-sheikh-each-night-put-kashmir-in-your-dreams
17. Devjyot Ghoshal, Fayaz Bukhari, 'Thousands Protest in Indian Kashmir over New Status despite Clampdown', Reuters, 9 August 2019.
18. Vijayta Lalwani, '"A Country without a Post Office": In Kashmir, postal services remain suspended for two weeks', Scroll.in, 20 August 2019.
19. 'About 4,000 People Arrested in Kashmir since August 5: Govt Sources to AFP', *The Hindu*, 18 August 2019.
20. Agha Shahid Ali, 'The Blessed Word', *The Veiled Suite*.
21. Mirza Waheed, 'How to Award a Posthumous Sedition Award to a Poet', Scroll.in, 16 February 2016.
22. Ather Zia, personal interview, February 2021.
23. Ibid.
24. On February 2020, the Trinamool Congress MP Mahua Moitra quoted from 'Farewell' during her speech in the Lok Sabha condemning the Citizenship Amendment Act. See, 'Real Guardian of Our Constitution: TMC MP Mahua Moitra's Viral Lok Sabha Speech Wins Twitter' (video), Scroll.in, 4 February 2020.
25. Abhishek Saha, 'Twitter Laughs Out Loud as JNU Row Inspires RTI Application', *Hindustan Times*, 21 February 2016.
26. Ashutosh Bhardwaj and Apurva, 'Parliament Watch: Quoting Wisdom from 40 BC, Misquoting Kashmiri Poet', *Indian Express*, 25 February 2016.
27. Abhishek Saha, 'Twitter Laughs Out Loud as JNU Row Inspires RTI Application'.
28. Deborah Klenotic, 'A Surprisingly Cheerful Chronicler of Dismemberment: Poet and Professor Agha Shahid Ali and *The Country without a Post Office*', *UMass Inside*, Spring 1998.

Illustration Credits

Illustration 1: Agha Shahid Ali Literary Trust
Illustration 2: Agha Shahid Ali Literary Trust
Illustration 3: Agha Shahid Ali Literary Trust
Illustration 4: Agha Shahid Ali Literary Trust
Illustration 5: Agha Shahid Ali Literary Trust
Illustration 6: Agha Shahid Ali Literary Trust
Illustration 7: Courtesy: Saleem Kidwai
Illustration 8: Courtesy: Saleem Kidwai
Illustration 9: Agha Shahid Ali Archives, Burke Library, Hamilton College, New York
Illustration 10: Agha Shahid Ali Archives, Burke Library, Hamilton College, New York
Illustration 11: Agha Shahid Ali Archives, Burke Library, Hamilton College, New York
Illustration 12: Agha Shahid Ali Archives, Burke Library, Hamilton College, New York
Illustration 13: Agha Shahid Ali Archives, Burke Library, Hamilton College, New York
Illustration 14: *James Merrill Papers, Julian Edison Department of Special Collections, Washington University Libraries*
Illustration 15: Agha Shahid Ali Literary Trust
Illustration 16: Photographer: Neil Davenport, courtesy: Agha Shahid Ali Archives, Burke Library, Hamilton College, New York

Illustration 17: Photographer: Kevin Bubriski, courtesy:
AramcoWorld
Illustration 18: Agha Shahid Ali Literary Trust
Illustration 19: Agha Shahid Ali Literary Trust
Illustration 20: Agha Iqbal Ali
Illustration 21: Izhar Patkin
Illustration 22: Izhar Patkin
Illustration 23: Izhar Patkin
Illustration 24: Masood Hussain
Illustration 25: Masood Hussain

Text Credits

'I Dream I Am at the Ghat of the Only World', Copyright © 2002 by Agha Shahid Ali. 'Snow on the Desert', Copyright © 1991 by Agha Shahid Ali. 'Today, talk is cheap. Call somebody.', Copyright © 1987 by Agha Shahid Ali. 'I Dream I Return to Tucson in the Monsoons', Copyright © 1991 by Agha Shahid Ali. 'Phil was afraid of being forgotten.', Copyright © 1991 by Agha Shahid Ali. 'When on Route 80 in Ohio', Copyright © 1991 by Agha Shahid Ali. 'Tonight', Copyright © 2003 by Agha Shahid Ali Literary Trust. 'In Arabic', Copyright © 2003 by Agha Shahid Ali Literary Trust. 'The Blessed Word: A Prologue', Copyright © 1997 by Agha Shahid Ali. 'The Correspondent', Copyright © 1997 by Agha Shahid Ali. 'After an August Wedding in Lahore', Copyright © 1997 by Agha Shahid Ali. 'Lenox Hill', Copyright © 2002 by Agha Shahid Ali. 'Above the Cities', Copyright © 2002 by Agha Shahid Ali. 'Karbala: A History of the House of Sorrow', Copyright © 2002 by Agha Shahid Ali. 'The Veiled Suite', 'Air', Copyright © 2003 by Agha Shahid Ali Literary Trust. 'The Last Saffron', Copyright © 1997 by Agha Shahid Ali. 'By the Waters of the Sind', Copyright © 2002 by Agha Shahid Ali. From THE VEILED SUITE: THE COLLECTED POEMS by Agha Shahid Ali. Copyright © 2009 by the Agha Shahid Ali Literary Trust. Used by permission of W. W. Norton & Company, Inc.

Excerpt from 'Two Tramps in Mud Time' by Robert Frost from THE POETRY OF ROBERT FROST edited by Edward Connery Lathem. Copyright © 1969 by Henry Holt and Company. Copyright © 1936 by

4 lines from 'Postcard from Kashmir', 8 lines from 'The Seasons of the Plains', 9 lines from 'Snowmen', 5 lines from 'Prayer Rug', 2 lines from 'Flight from Houston in January', 8 lines from 'After Seeing Kozintsev's King Lear in Delhi', 15 lines from 'The Dacca Gauzes', and 8 lines from 'Homage to Faiz Ahmad Faiz' from *The Half-Inch Himalayas* © 1987 by Agha Shahid Ali. Published by Wesleyan University Press. Used by permission.

Excerpts from 'The Walled City: Seven Poems on Delhi', 'Note Autobiographical—2', 'At Jama Masjid, Delhi', and 'Qawwali at Nizamuddin Aulia's Dargah', from *In Memory of Begum Akhtar* by Agha Shahid Ali (1979). Originally published by Writers Workshop, Kolkata, India.

Agha Shahid Ali, letter to James Merrill, 30 September 1990, from Special Collections, Burke Library, Hamilton College, Clinton, New York.

Agha Shahid Ali, Application to Ball State, Special Collections, Burke Library, Hamilton College.

Index